Historical Anthology
of
Kazan Tatar Verse

Historical Anthology of Kazan Tatar Verse

Voices of Eternity

Edited and Translated by

David J. Matthews and Ravil Bukharaev

LONDON AND NEW YORK

First Published in 2000
by Curzon Press

Published 2016 by Routledge
2 Park Square, Milton Park, Abingdon, Oxfordshire OX14 4RN
711 Third Avenue, New York, NY 10017, USA

First issued in paperback 2016

Routledge is an imprint of the Taylor and Francis Group, an informa business

Editorial Matter © 2000 David J. Matthews and Ravil Bukharaev

Typeset in Centaur by LaserScript Ltd, Mitcham, Surrey

All rights reserved. No part of this book may be reprinted or reproduced or utilised in any form or by any electronic, mechanical, or other means, now known or hereafter invented, including photocopying and recording, or in any information storage or retrieval system, without permission in writing from the publishers.

British Library Cataloguing in Publication Data
A catalogue record of this book is available from the British Library

ISBN 13: 978-1-138-99222-1 (pbk)
ISBN 13: 978-0-7007-1077-5 (hbk)

Contents

Preface	x
List of Illustrations	xiii
A Note on Transcription	xv
A Note on the Translation	xvii
Map of the Region	xx
HISTORICAL INTRODUCTION	1
Volga-Bulgaria (before 1236)	1
The Rise and Fall of the Golden Horde (1256–1400)	11
The Kazan Khanate (1436–1552)	18
Tatar Poetry of the Russian Empire (18th–19th Centuries)	25
The Lake of Swans	36
VOLGA-BULGARIA TO THE GOLDEN HORDE:	
12th–14th CENTURIES	41
Kol Gali (Qul ʿAlī) (1183–1236)	41
The dream of Malik	41
The conclusion of the poem	46
The poem of Edighey (14th century)	48
Hisam Kyatib (14th century)	51
The Skull King	51
Anonymous (14th century)	63
The Severed Head	63
Saif-i Sarai (c. 1321–1396)	71
The Dawn Qasīda	71
Ghazals	73
THE KAZAN KHANATE: 15th–17th CENTURIES	75
Muhammad Amin (Amīn) (1460–1518)	75
The calamity	75

Ömmi Kamal *(second half of the 15th century)*   76
    Spring   76
Kol Sharif *(d. 1552)*   77
    Ghazal   77
Muhammedyar, also known as Mahmūd Khojī *(16th century)*   78
    The fate of a girl   78
    On goodness   82
    A dialogue between the poet and his heart   82
    A husband and wife who spun and sold their yarn   84
    On generosity   89
Mevla *(Maulā)* Koly *(17th century)*   90
    On tramps   90
    Love, passion and morality   90
    On kinsmen   91
    This world   91
    Preface to the *Hikmet*   91
    On rich people   92

THE RUSSIAN EMPIRE: 18th–19th CENTURIES   93
    Gabderrahim ('Abdurrahīm) Utyz Imyani *(1754–1836)*   93
        What it means to be a Jigit   93
        Friendship   94
        Munajat   95
        From 'Advice on the cleansing of the thoughts'   96
        From 'The gifts of time'   98
    Abelmanikh Kargaly *(1782–1833?)*   101
        A wasted life   101
        Ignorance   101
    Hibatullah Salikhov *(1794–1867)*   103
        A tale with a moral   103
    Gabdeljabbar ('Abdul Jabbār) Kandaly *(1797–1860)*   107
        The mulla and his wife   107
        From 'Sahibjamal'   108
    Gali ('Alī) Chokri *(1826–1889)*   112
        The sacking of Bolgar   112
        In praise of Kazan   114
        Lines on his own verse   114
    Yakov Yemelyanov *(1848–1893)*   115
        Grief   115
        A poor life   116

Slander	117
Arrogance	118
Gabdulla ('Abdullāh) Tukai (1886–1913)	119
The Haymarket	119
The Shuraleh	132
Muhammad Zakir Rameev 'Derdmend' (1895–1921)	140
I could not even sprinkle my pale shroud	140
My only hope is Allah	141
Autumn	142
The ship	142
Sometimes	143
Sagit Rameev (1880–1926)	144
Deceived	144

SOVIET AND CONTEMPORARY VERSE
FROM 1917 ONWARDS

	146
Hadi Taktash (1901–1931)	146
The angels of death	146
On a dark night	148
Consolation	148
Kazan	150
Zagira (Za'ira) Baichurina (1880–1962)	153
Flax	153
Temptation	154
Iffat Tutash (Zahida Burnasheva) (1895–1977)	156
The Volga	156
I search	156
To the heart	157
Hasan Tufan (1900–1981)	159
Storm, do not abate	159
The storm	159
But even so we trust and wait	161
But just suppose he comes one day	161
The Caspian shore	162
Not to leave	162
Tomb	163
Musa Jalil (1906–1944)	164
The first rain	164
Poet	165
My songs	166
Obsessive thoughts	167

The last song	167
The bell	168
Fatih Karim (1900–1945)	169
Autumn rain	169
Snowdrop	169
Sibgat Hakim (1911–1986)	171
Why does war persist in haunting me?	171
Go off to England!	171
Lebyazhe in the autumn	172
Light and shade	172
Thirst	172
Nuri Arslanov (1912–1991)	174
At times	174
Ahmed Yerikei (1902–1967)	175
Sumbul	175
The Lacemaker	175
You and I are not the same	176
Enver Davydov (1919–1968)	177
Love	177
My pen	178
Sajida Suleimanova (1926–1980)	179
Through the years	179
Shaukat Galiev (b. 1933)	180
My generation	180
Road	180
I can suffer any hardship	180
Ahsan Bayanov (b. 1930)	181
By the Minaret	181
Ildar Yuzeev (b. 1933)	182
Raven	182
The setting sun	182
O greenness of the meadows	182
Ballad of sadness	183
Klara Bulatova (b. 1936)	187
You went astray	187
Rustam Mingalimov (b. 1937)	188
Meditations	188
The river of childhood	188
Rustem Kutui (b. 1936)	189
Swallow	189

Robert Ahmetzhanov (b. 1935)	190
My son, take this book	190
Elegy	190
Ravil Faizullin (b. 1943)	191
On Bolgar	191
Snow and verdure	191
The blind sun of the domes	191
The sky	192
Shadow theatre	192
Radif Gatash (Gataullin) (b. 1941)	193
Other girls were dancing	193
Farewell	193
Melody of memories	194
Garai Rahim (b. 1938)	195
Generations	195
Oaks of my native-land	195
Root	196
On a bus	197
Still here the snowy fields	198
Renat Haris (b. 1941)	199
Window casings	199
The felling of the elm	200
I touched a cloud	201
Ahmed 'Adil (b. 1942)	202
Doves	202
Mudarris Aglyamov (b. 1946)	203
Ah! Why Creator?	203
Zulfat (b. 1947)	204
Horses bathing	204
Flight of the soul	204
Razil Valeev (b. 1947)	205
Fire in the Museum of Local Lore	205
Heathen	206
Robert Minnullin (b. 1948)	207
The Wave of the River Syun	207
Fannur Safin (1948–1992)	208
Snowdrop	208
Ravil Bukharaev (b. 1951)	209
Bee	209

Preface

My path is narrow, but my way is straight;
My people are Tatars; I shall not fear.
                                    G. Tukai

I am Tatar and the son of a Tatar.
If you say otherwise my friend, beware!
                                    Derdmend

For many people the former Soviet Union was always something of an enigma. From time immemorial this vast area of the world has been inhabited by hundreds of larger and smaller nations, all of them having their own native tongues, folklore and literature. Yet few people have been aware of the considerable variety of the cultures and languages which have existed and indeed still exist in what was termed the USSR. Whatever emerged from the country was usually thought of merely as 'Russian'. Little attention was paid to the non-Slavonic communities, which made up a very large part of its population.

This Anthology aims at providing an illustrated account of the largely unknown verse of just one of these nations, the Kazan Tatars, a people who have inhabited the regions along the Volga for over a thousand years. Their language, which belongs to the Uralian or Kipchak-Bulgar division of the modern Turkic languages, has been written since at least the middle of the 13th century AD, and its literature, mainly in the form of verse, has continued to flourish often against all odds to the present day. According to the population census of 1979, 6.3 million Soviet citizens recorded their nationality as 'Tatar', making them the third largest Turkic group and the sixth in the rank order of Soviet nationalities. Their historical home, Tatarstan, is now a Presidential Republic within the framework of the

Russian Federation, with which it maintains a bilateral treaty of association. Its capital city, Kazan, has for a long time been its main political and cultural centre, and like its inhabitants it has miraculously survived the destruction periodically inflicted upon it by its attackers.

The earliest major text, the language of which we can feel justified in calling 'Tatar', is a lengthy and ornate adaptation of the Quranic story of Joseph, versions of which are also found in Persian and other languages. The *Kitāb-i Yūsuf*, 'The Book of Joseph', was written during the 13th century by a certain Kol Gali (Qul 'Alī) who probably died during the attack on the Volga city of Bolgar by the armies of Chingīz Khān in 1236. From the point of view of style and versification the work is quite remarkable, and as the first substantial work of Tatar literature holds a special place in the affections of its people. Like much of the Tatar literature which followed it, the 'Book of Joseph' survived mainly by chance. The Mongol invasions of the Volga regions dispersed the indigenous population, which only with the greatest difficulty managed to preserve at least a part of its culture.

During the period of the Golden Horde, which lasted for almost two centuries, other Tatar poets emerged, producing versions of well-known tales such as the 'Skull King' and the 'Severed Head'. In these stories, the skull and the disembodied head deliver grave warnings to the reader about the folly of pride and the trials that await sinners in the life to come. These moralistic legends, which have often been retold, though naive, and in parts quite amusing, provide us with almost the only written evidence we possess for the reaction of the Tatars to life under the Mongol Yoke. The verse literature of this long and harrowing period reached its climax with the lyric poetry of Saif-i Sarai, who was forced to flee before his country was once more overrun, this time by the ruthless onslaught of Tamerlane in 1388. Yet again the cities of the Tatars along with their libraries and places of learning were destroyed.

History often repeated itself. In 1552, the Tatar capital, Kazan, fell to Ivan the Terrible, and much of its culture, which had temporarily revived, was erased. During the reigns of Peter the Great and Catherine, enforced conversion to Orthodoxy and the policy of 'Russification' not only robbed the Tatars of the right to practise their religion, Islam, but almost succeeded in eradicating their language. The literature we have from the 18th century was largely the product of village *madrasas*, traditional Islamic schools which were practically the only source of education for the majority of the people. Tatars were forbidden to settle in their former towns, and, unless they became Christian, were also deprived of their land. From this time onwards, exile and alienation from what the people viewed as a glorious past became one of the major themes of their poetry.

Even in the more liberal atmosphere of the 19th century, Tatar writers had to struggle for their cultural survival, and so many of them died prematurely in poverty. No sooner had the first printing-press been established in Kazan than the revolutions of 1905 and 1917 plunged the land once more into chaos. The Stalinist repression of minorities was so harsh that it is remarkable that their spirit survived. The script of the language was changed twice – from Arabic to Roman, and then to Cyrillic. Censorship was, of course, harshly imposed. During the first decades of the 20th century, Tatar poets, like their Russian contemporaries, spoke much of the devastation and futility of war, the glory of the motherland and the natural beauty of their own forests and fields.

Poetry still remains one of the most popular means of self-expression among the Tatars, and modern newspapers frequently contain whole pages devoted to it. With the recent formation of Tatarstan, writers have begun to feel that after many centuries of deprivation they at last have a land in which they will be able to give free rein to their thoughts and talents.

In this book, we have tried to present through English translation a picture of what Tatar poets have contributed to the world over the last eight centuries. Because of the ravages of history much of what was written has been lost, and indeed a great deal more research remains to be done. We are sadly aware that our selection represents little more than a fragment of what might have existed.

This book was originally conceived by Ravil Bukharaev, who contributed much of the historical information contained in the Introduction, and selected the poems included in the Anthology. Ravil Bukharaev also made a word-for-word translation of the anthology from Tatar into English. The final editing and the rendering of the Tatar poems into English verse were the responsibility of David Matthews.

We wish to express our gratitude to President Mintimer Shaimiev and to the Government of the Republic of Tatarstan for the generous support they gave in making this work possible.

David J. Matthews
Ravil Bukharaev

List of Illustrations

Plates appear between pages 76 and 77

People
1. A Bulgar, 8th – 9th centuries
2. A Kazan Tatar, 15th – 17th centuries
3. A Kazan townswoman, mid-16th century
4. Old painting of Queen Suyumbika and her son. The man in the background is believed to be the poet Mukhammedyar.
5. A Kazan Tatar, 18th century
6. A Kazan Tatar, 19th century
7. Art Nouveau style costume of a Kazan Tatar, beginning of the 20th century

Calligraphy
8. Samples of fine calligraphy, a Persian Divan, 1800s
9. Frontispiece of a mid-19th century manuscript by calligrapher Ali Makhmudov
10. Ornamental headpiece in watercolour for a 19th century Qur'an
11. Manuscript page by calligrapher Ali Makhmudov and an advertisement prospectus by V. Varaksin (right), mid-19th century
12. Samples of shamail wall panels by calligrapher G. Saliev, beginning of the 20th century

Architecture
13. The Smaller Minaret of Bolgar the Great, 14th century
14. The Black Chamber, believed to be a school or some other public institution of Bolgar the Great, 14th century
15. The Khan's Tomb or the Eastern Mausoleum of Bolgar the Great, 14th century
16. 'Kazan of Old', oil painting by Ravil Zagidullin
17. The Azimov Mosque in Kazan, built 1887–90
18. The minaret of the Azimov Mosque in Kazan
19. The Hay Market Mosque of Kazan, built in 1849

Artifacts of the 19th century

20 Kazan Tatar belt-buckle in gold filigree
21 Section of foliate belt-buckle, set with jewels
22 Silvergilt collar pendent in open-work filigree
23 Ajoure silvergilt brooch with triple foliate pendants
24 Napkin worked with coloured silks in chain stitch
25 Tablecloth corner worked with coloured silks in chain stitch
26 *Orpek* national head covering, embroidery in chain stitch
27 Velver skullcap with tassel, worked with chain-stitched gold thread, bullion, twisted metal wire and paillettes

A Note on Transcription

Until the first decades of the 20th century, Tatar was written in an adapted version of the Arabic alphabet. In the 1920s, the script was romanized by government order, but subsequently was brought into line with the other Turkic languages of the Soviet Union by being written in an augmented version of the Cyrillic (i.e. Russian) script. The latter is still used for writing Tatar. None of these scripts or orthographic systems are totally adequate for representing the sounds of the language, and further reforms, inclining in favour of a new Roman script, are at present under review. Transcription therefore presents some problems.

The Arabic alphabet for the most part consists only of consonants, some of which are also used to represent long vowels. (This inadequacy led to Mustafa Kemal's reform of Turkish orthography in the early part of this century.) The signs for three of the short vowels, /a/, /i/, /u/ are rarely used. This is naturally a great disadvantage when writing Turkic languages, which possess a far wider range of vowels than Arabic. Moreover, the pronunciation of certain Arabic consonants, which are of common occurrence in Tatar and other Turkic languages, also differs considerably from that of Arabic. For example, the Arabic pharyngeal fricative *ain*, which we transcribe as /ᶜ/, in Tatar is pronounce as /g/. Thus the name, commonly transcribed from Arabic as *Ali*, is pronounced roughly as *Gali* in Tatar.

In Cyrillic, the sound /h/, which is represented by two different letters in the Arabic alphabet (as in Hasan, Hārūn etc,) is written as /x/, which in Russian is pronounced as the /ch/ in the Scottish *loch*. We prefer *Hasan* to the commonly transcribed *Khasan*.

When transliterating proper names, we have given them first in the form which represents contemporary Tatar pronunciation. This is followed by the form of name as it is written in the Arabic alphabet, and the one which will be more familiar to the western reader. Thus the name *Kol Gali* is followed in brackets by its Arabic-alphabet version *Qul 'Alī*. Similarly *Gabdeljabbar* is followed by *'Abdul-Jabbār*, etc.

The following conventions are followed in this book:

(i) vowels marked with a macron are pronounced long:

/ā/ as in English 'father'   e.g. *Kātib*
/ī/ as in English 'seem'   e.g. *Chingīz*
/ū/ as in English 'soon'   e.g. *Rūmī*

(ii) the transcription of the following consonants should also be noted:

/j/ as in English 'judge'   e.g. *Jochi*
/kh/ as in Scottish 'loch'   e.g. *Khān*
/q/ as in English 'king'   e.g. *Qāzi*
/ᶜ/ Arabic *'ain*   ignored in pronunciation, e.g. *'Alī*
/gh/ is a 'voiced' *kh*   e.g. *ghazal*

Double consonants are given their full force as in Italian *giubba, ecco*, etc., e.g. *Jabbār*.

The above remarks apply mainly to names cited in the Introduction, the short biographical notices which precede each selection, and the footnotes. Names in the text of the poems are given without diacritics. When place-names have commonly accepted English spellings, such as Mecca, Medina, Kerbala etc., these have been retained.

The Persian (and indeed Tatar) spellings *Chingīz Khān* and *Tīmur* are used throughout for the common English variants: 'Genghis Khan' and 'Taimur' or 'Tamerlane'.

Finally it should be noted that the spelling *Bolgar* is used for the name of the city, while *Bulgar* denotes the region and its people.

A Note on the Translation

From the earliest period, Tatar verse, like that of Arabic and Persian, and indeed later of Russian, has for the most part been rhymed and written in accordance with strict rules of prosody and metre. 'Blank verse', composed with no detectable or regular rhythm and rhyme, even among modern writers, is a rare exception. When translating Tatar verse into English, therefore, we have done our best to reflect this tradition.

Poets who wrote before, during and immediately after the time of the Golden Horde used either traditional Turkish rhythms, such as the popular hendecasyllable (i.e. lines containing eleven syllables), or metres closely based on the quantitive system employed in Arabic and Persian. Like the metres of Ancient Greek and Latin verse those of Arabic and Persian conform to patterns of long and short syllables, and not as in English to those involving stress. Such metres were codified by using various forms of the basic Arabic verb *fiʻl* 'to do'. Thus the popular metre $^-\cup^-{}^-|^-\cup^-{}^-|^-\cup^-{}^-|^-\cup^-{}^-$, known technically by the name *ramal* (three feet with the pattern: long, long, short, long, and the fourth foot: long, short, long), would be noted by the formula: *fāʻilātun, fāʻilātun, fāʻilātun, fāʻilun*. This is in fact the metre of the poem *Kisek-bash* 'The Severed Head' and reference to the somewhat cumbersome system of notation is made jokingly by Tukai in the last verse of his poem *The Haymarket*. Once such a metrical pattern is established in the first verse of the poem, no variation can be admitted.

These traditional metres persisted long after the collapse of the Golden Horde and can still be found in the verse of modern poets by whom they have been revived. During the 18th and 19th centuries, however, the influence of Russian prosody is obvious and the rhythms become a combination of both stress and quantity.

Rhyme also plays a large part in Tatar verse. Many of the long narrative poems, like classical Persian *masnavīs*, are composed in rhyming couplets. Some like the *Qissa-e Yūsuf* have the rhyme scheme AAAX, BBBX etc., with the last words of the fourth line being repeated in each stanza. The *qasīda* (like the *Dawn Ode* of Saif-i Sarai) and the *ghazal* (the short lyric), a favourite genre of many poets, have the rhyme scheme AA, BA, CA etc. Later Tatar poetry is rhymed in much the same way as its contemporary Russian verse, a popular pattern being ABAB etc.

It is, of course, impossible to imitate rhythm and rhyme exactly, since most of the traditional patterns are quite alien to the English ear. We have, therefore, often been obliged to compromise, and, while retaining rhythm and rhyme, have chosen forms which fit more naturally into English verse.

In translating the Tatar texts we have tried to reflect the original as faithfully and accurately as possible, but have made no attempt to imitate archaisms and *recherché* vocabulary, in which much of the earlier verse abounds. Our preference has been for modern, poetic English, which does justice to the original without becoming unnecessarily quaint.

The vast majority of the poems we have selected speak for themselves, and except for occasional footnotes, which for the most part gloss proper names or technical terms, we have added no learned or dreary commentary.

While preparing this Anthology, we became acutely aware that little background material on Tatar literature exists elsewhere. The majority of the texts we have chosen exist only in small volumes which are now out of print. A certain amount of excellent research has been conducted by modern Tatar scholars, and such work is now proceeding apace. Translations of some of the works of the best known writers are available in Russian, but the availability of such books is severely limited. Little mention of the poets who flourished in Volga-Bulgaria is made even in the best histories of Turkish literature, whose authors are presumably unaware of their existence. The epic poem of *Edighey* and the *Suhail-Geldersen* romance of Saif-i Sarai, for example, are surely worthy of much deeper study.

By offering this small selection of Tatar verse in English translation we hope to have done some justice to a largely unknown literature which certainly deserves its rightful place in the world.

In the selection, the poets have been introduced in chronological order. Four major divisions have been made: (1) poets who lived before and during the Golden Horde; (2) poets of the Kazan Khanate; (3) poets of the Russian Empire which came to an end with the Revolution of 1917 and (4) contemporary poets, all of whom were born and/or worked during the Soviet period. Brief biographies have been given for those poets who have gained a lasting national reputation. Contemporary writers are referred to only by their dates.

Map of the Region

Historical Introduction: Volga-Bulgaria (before 1236)

> *Your every stone, fit for a precious ring,*
> *Will fill my soul with pride for its true art.*
> *Ah, Bolgar! You are not a simple song;*
> *You are the very centre of my heart*
>   Renat Haris

If we look at a map of the area which extends from the Volga to the Urals and consider the movements throughout history of the peoples who have traversed it and brought to it their various cultures, we begin to appreciate that this region, in spite of its apparent remoteness from the better studied centres of human civilization, was never, as some have imagined, 'a God-forsaken and miserable land'. It was crossed from east to west by the White and Black Huns who emerged from the depths of Siberia, and by traders who sought both goods and knowledge. From the most ancient times trade routes extended from north to south facilitating access to fur, silver and gold which abounded in the region. In his account of Heracles and Gelonos, Herodotus mentions a wooden city[1], which was situated somewhere on the southern frontier of the Hyperborean lands. By some it is thought that this city stood near the mouth of the river Kama, which flows into the Volga where the city of Bolgar was later constructed. If this is correct, the territory of Volga-Bulgaria, the centre of Tatar civilization and literature, would have been exposed to Greek culture as early as the fifth century B.C.

    In Turkic languages the Volga is variously called *Itil* (Old Turkish), *Idel* (Kazan Tatar) and *Atil* (Chuvash), and the name is popularly connected with that of Attila. The Russian name Volga has a number of popular etymologies ranging from Turkic *elga* 'river' to

'Valhalla', the paradise of the gods of the Vikings who sailed along its stream.

Whatever the truth of the many fanciful or even possible accounts and hypotheses, we can say with certainty that the present day Republic of Tatarstan, which roughly covers the central area of the once illustrious Volga-Bulgaria, has always been a meeting place for various cultures and civilisations of the world. Fur from the Urals was worn by the rulers of ancient Greece, Babylon, Persia and India as well as by the monarchs of Byzantium. Traders not only exchanged goods, but brought with them the cultural traditions of their own lands, and such memories were preserved and reflected in the legends which grew up in the Volga-Ural area. Traces of these legends can be found in literatures as far apart as those of Finland, Hungary, Northern China and Siberia. The myth of the Eternal Tree, which extends its branches to the heavenly abode of the gods is found in the folklore of both Tatarstan and Scandinavia.

Volga-Tatar, or Kazan Tatar, as the language of our poetry is often called, belongs to the group of Turkic languages, the earliest written evidence for which dates from the sixth to eighth centuries AD. The first phases of 'Turkic' literature are usually regarded as the common property of all the Turks; later phases, which reflect the ethnic and cultural peculiarities of the various national groups, form separate literatures. Turkish, however, is noted for its 'conservatism' and the modern branches of the language have remained very close to each other. Those who know contemporary Turkish, therefore, will have little difficulty in coming to terms with Tatar, Uzbek or Kazakh, though it would be a gross exaggeration to say that these languages are mutually comprehensible[2].

When we search for the earliest traces of Kazan Tatar poetry, we should base our observations on geographical and cultural distinctions rather than linguistic factors. In as much as it is difficult to separate the various Turkic languages in the earliest stages of their development, it will be reasonable to define Tatar writing as that which was composed in the region where those who thought of themselves as Tatars actually lived and worked. This means the area that was usually known as Volga-Bulgaria.

Few ancient geographical names have survived since the first appearance of the 'Bulgars' in the region between the Volga and Kama rivers. The names *Bolgar* and *Idel*, however, are found on the oldest maps, such as the Roger Map of Al-Idrīsī, which was made in Sicily in 1154 AD. These maps were based on the accounts of early travellers who visited Bolgar in the 9th and 10th centuries. The narratives of Ibn-Fadlan, Ibn Haukal and Al-Masʿūdī were followed by the account of the Andalusian traveller, Al-Gharnāti who visited the city of Bolgar several times between 1135 and 1151. Al-Gharnāti made extensive use of local historical sources, one of them being a history of Bolgar by Ibn Nogman (Ibn Nuʿmān), the former Qāzi of the city. From this book, which is now lost, he quotes:

> *Once a Muslim merchant, well versed in medical studies, came to Bolgar from Bukhara. At the time, the king of Bolgar and his wife were very ill and had lost all hope of recovery. In spite of employing the local remedies, they were deteriorating and already feared imminent death. The holy-man asked them if they would accept his faith. Both agreed, saying "Yes we shall." After the holy-man had given them the appropriate cure, the King and his wife recovered and embraced the faith of Islam*[3].

It is known that Islam came to the Volga-Kama region towards the middle of the ninth century. Ibn Rusta in his 'Book of Noble Treasures' which was compiled between 903 and 907 AD records that the King of Bolgar and his family and courtiers were Muslim. He also mentions the existence in local townships and villages of mosques, schools, *mullahs* and *muezzins*, and states that the King wages 'holy wars' on his pagan neighbours.

The date 922 AD is commonly accepted for the 'official' arrival of Islam on the banks of the middle Volga. Along with the introduction of Islamic tenets came a sharp increase in literacy, and these factors greatly improved the trade relations of Volga-Bulgaria with the rest of the Islamic world. The region now became part of the cultural sphere embraced by the more advanced civilisations of Khwarezm, Persia, the Arab Middle East and Spain. So far the Turks had played a minor role in the Islamic world, and Volga-Bulgaria might be considered one of the first Turkic states having all the components and potential of a highly developed urban culture. The population of the area was made up not only of the ancient Bulgar and Kipchak tribes, but also inhabited by people of Finno-Ugric origin[4]. Slav tribes, fleeing from the compulsory baptism which they were forced to undergo in Rus', added to the ethnic mosaic. A seventeenth century Russian treatise, which describes the conquered Tatar territories clearly states:

> *'There live Khazars, Balyms (?) and Bulgars as well as some fugitives from lands of Rostov, who, having rejected Holy Baptism for their paganism, have*

taken refuge in Tatar territory and embraced Islam along with their nomadic way of life[5].

The predominant component of the Volga-Bulgar population, however, remained Turkic, and their language remained their own branch of Turkish. In 'The Collection of the Languages of the Turks', compiled by Mahmūd Kāshgarī around 1170 AD, we find the first poetic reference to the river *Itil*, the Volga:

The Itil's stream will ever flow;
Against the cliffs will ever blow
And fish and frogs will live and grow
And water-meadows overflow.

This simple poem, which may be ascribed to the tenth century or even earlier, perhaps a remnant of ancient folk literature, is written in a metre still used by Kazan Tatars. Although there are no real grounds for claiming it to be the very first piece of Tatar verse we possess, and indeed other Turkic-speaking people might be justified in making the same claim for themselves, the mention of the Volga has led some to conclude that it is indeed Tatar!

During the eleventh and twelfth centuries, before the Mongol invasion, which began in earnest in 1236 AD, Volga-Bulgaria appears to have been prosperous in both material and cultural terms. In his work *Islam and the Soviet Union*, Alexandre Bennigsen refers to the Tatars of the Volga as 'possessors of an ancient and splendid civilisation'[6]. We may judge the achievements of that period on both archaeological finds and written works composed in the Middle East and other parts of the world. Although accounts mentioning the Tatars contain no examples of any verse that might have been written at the time, the mention of the names of certain authors suggest that a literature may have existed.

We have already mentioned Yaqūb ibn Nuʿmān (1022–1086), the Qāzi of Bolgar, and his history from which al-Gharnāti quoted. In addition we know of the existence of a certain Hoja Ahmed Bolgari, who according to some sources, was employed as a teacher by Mahmud Ghaznavī (907–1030)[7]. Other names include Abul 'Alā Hamīd bin Idrīs al Bolgari, who flourished at the beginning of the twelfth century, the scholars and poets Sulaimān bin Daud, Borhanetdin Ibrahim Bolgari (d.1204), and Tajetdin bin Yunus al-Bolgari. All of them lived and worked in the cities of Volga-Bulgaria, such as Bolgar the Great, Suwar, Saksin and Juketau, where silver coins were minted from the middle of the tenth century. The following two lines engraved on a coin of Bolgar dating from 930 AD were actually included in the latest anthology of Tatar poetry[8]:

> Minted in the city of Bolgar
> By Mikail bine Ja'far[9]

Through their trade the Turkic-speaking inhabitants of the whole region maintained close contact. Merchants from Bulgar to Khwarezm as well as Sufi preachers from Central Asia travelled the vast expanses of the Kipchak Steppe – the *Dasht-i Kipchak*. Turkish in its varying colloquial forms and the verse composed in the language were understood by all.

One of the first 'classical' Turkish poets, whose influence has persisted over the centuries, was the Sufi Hoja Ahmed Yasavī (d.1166)[10]. He was born to a family of shaikhs, studied in Bukhara and later became the founder of his own Sufi order, the Yasaviya. His verse played an important role in spreading not only his own brand of mysticism but Islamic ideas in general to all corners of the *Dasht-i Kipchak*. In his poetry he staunchly defended the use of 'Türki' in place of Fārsī, Persian, which was the more widely accepted medium for literary composition:

> *The learned do not welcome you, our halting Turkish speech*
> *Yet in the mouths of scholars it shows riches of the soul.*

> *Poor, hapless Hoja Ahmad, may your ancestors be praised*
> *The one well-versed in Farsi knows the worth of the Turkish tongue.*

The very idea that the everyday spoken language might become a medium for poetic expression seemed revolutionary in the middle of the eleventh century, and the debate between advocates of Arabic and Persian and the use of literary vocabulary taken over from these languages versus the plain Kazan *lingua franca* has been going on ever since.

In any literature one looks for the appearance of a figure of undeniable worth and stature whose work constitutes the true beginning of the classical age; a poet or writer one can honour as being the founder of a solid tradition of national literature. Such a figure is Kol Gali (Qul 'Alī) whose long poem *Kitāb-i Yūsuf* or *Qissa-i Yūsuf*, 'The Book of Yusuf' or 'The Story of Yusuf' was probably completed in 1233 AD/630 AH. The oldest existing manuscript of the poem is now in the Dresden Library[11]. Other manuscripts, which originate from Kazan and villages near Kazan are preserved in St. Petersburg, Ufa, Baku and Berlin, and some 120 copies are at present in Kazan itself.

There can be little dispute about the language of the poem which in many respects resembles that spoken in present-day Kazan, naturally with a considerable stock of words taken from Arabic and Persian, which have now become obsolete. The poem has remained constantly popular through the ages and it later became an important textbook used for improving the reading skills of Tatar children and adults alike. It is always been widely known and in a list of the possessions which during the Pugachev uprising of 1774 were confiscated from one Nādir Sharīf figures a copy of the 'Book of Yusuf'[12]. Another document testifies to a gold-bound volume of the *Book of Yusuf* being sold to a wealthy Tatar villager 'in front of some respected people'. It is significant that all the manuscripts of the poem originated only from the region historically inhabited by the Kazan Tatars who have long regarded the work as part of their literary heritage. The 'Book of Yusuf' has been committed to memory, sung, and, as is often the fate of inspired works of literature, has been used as a source for fortune-telling. Its influence on poets who came after Kol Gali is inestimable, and its metre, images and aphorisms have often been imitated and adapted. We are, therefore, completely justified in calling the 'Book of Yusuf' the first great masterpiece of Kazan-Tatar verse.

All we know for certain about the author, apart from the rough dates of his life, are the scant details, which are contained in the poem itself. The last section ends with the following verses:

Kol Gali is They servant's name, Oh Lord Benign;
With four and twenty syllables he made each line.
Forgive Thy slave; upon him shed Thy grace divine.
May he send me his mercy, which I hope for now.

In the year six-hundred and thirty was this work complete;
The thirtieth day of Rajab did my labours greet;
I made this shining vault of verse and poetry sweet.
And I received the grace of the Creator now.

The first part of the name of the author, Kol Gali is probably to be interpreted as 'slave (of God)', and the religious fervour expressed in the work suggests that he may have belonged to a Sufi order, perhaps that of Hoja Ahmed Yasavī or Sulaimān Bakyrgani, who also styled himself Kol Sulaiman[13].

Kol Sulaiman is a sinner as others are;
But still he clings to the hope of help from Thee.

Much work on the textual and historical analysis of the 'Book of Yusuf', which for many years was discouraged in the USSR, remains to be done. Recent research has shown that at various periods of his life Kol Gali resided and studied in several cities of Volga-Bulgaria and Khwarezm. He is also believed to have travelled to Persia and countries of the Middle East, most notably Syria and Egypt. Some scholars claim to have deduced from Tatar genealogical tables, *shajara*, that Kol Gali belonged to the royal line of Bolgar. It is, however, more probable that, like many Turkic poets, he came from a family of clerics, among whom scholarship and poetry prospered the most. Other theories suggest that he may have furthered his education at the *madrasa* of the Central Asian scholar Ibn Hājī and later spent several years teaching religious law in Khwarezm. Recently the Kazan archaeologist, Alfred Khalikov, has fixed his dates more precisely and states that he was born in 1183 and died between 1236 and 1240 during the Mongol invasion of Volga-Bulgaria[14]. However doubtful such precise dating may appear, it did not deter UNESCO from celebrating the 800th anniversary of the poet in 1983.

The fact that Kol Gali's poem is almost unknown in Central Asia suggests that, having been completed immediately prior to the Mongol onslaught, it became restricted to Volga-Bulgaria, the land of its origin. No other Turkic people has ever laid claim to it.

Based on the Quranic story of Joseph, versions of which are found in Persian and many other languages, the 'Story of Yusuf' shows the familiarity of the author with the traditions and customs of other Muslim countries such as Egypt (no doubt drawn from his reading of other works) but it also abounds in detailed description of the day-to-day life of the people of Volga-Bulgaria. Khalikov, for example, finds a striking similarity between the architecture of the King's palace of the Volga-Bulgar city of Bilyar and Kol Ali's description of the dream-palace contained in his work. Indeed it is argued that his last years were actually spent in Bilyar, where he may have died during the Mongol storm of the city.

It is a tragic coincidence that the Story of Yusuf marked not only the early genesis of Kazan Tatar poetry but also the end of the independent existence of the ancestors of the Kazan Tatars. If before this time the Tatars had roamed the world as traders and scholars at their own free will or at the will of their rulers, with the fall of Volga-Bulgaria to the Mongols their migration became a matter of compulsion. Here perhaps we can see the beginning of one of the most persistent themes of Kazan Tatar poetry: forced alienation from one's own land and its resulting nostalgia. Kol Gali's story of Joseph's capture and exile was written roughly at the same time as the anonymous Russian 'Lay of Igor's Host' and the 'Knight in the Tiger Skin' by the Georgian poet, Shota Rustaveli. No doubt inspired by Firdausi's version, his work places great emphasis on the inevitability of God's design, earthly peace and justice and the desire for a just ruler[15].

If Kol Gali was born around 1183 in Volga-Bulgaria, his life spanned a time of great troubles, when the people of the region were forced to struggle for their independent existence and compete for their markets with the neighbouring Russian principality of Vladimir-Suzdal. Russian-Bulgar relations had been generally good since 985 AD when, after a brief and almost bloodless encounter on the border a peace treaty had been concluded between Volga-Bulgaria and Kiev-Rus. Bulgars became trading partners and to some extent allies of the Kievan Princes and a relative feeling of security prevailed in the whole region for some 150 years. Things changed, however, at the beginning of the 12th century, when, with the decline of Kiev, Vladimir-Suzdal became the most dynamic principality of Rus. With the object of extending its sway along the Volga for almost the whole of the 12th century Vladimir-Suzdal waged war on the Bulgars, finally establishing its control over the Murom district, which the Bulgars had long since viewed as their own market. Decisive action aimed at squeezing Volga-Bulgaria from the left bank of the river was taken by Prince Andrei Bogolyubsky, who himself had Turkish blood in his veins and was married to a Bulgar princess.

During his lifetime, Kol Gali saw his own country split apart, rapidly approaching its fatal collapse. Wherever the poet resided, whether it was Khwarezm or some other country he would be sure to hear of yet another Russian attack on Volga-Bulgaria. The final blow came in 1204 AD with the capture of Constantinople by the combined forces of the Venetians and Crusaders. Of the subsequent plunder a Greek eyewitness Niketas wrote:

'The sacred altar, formed of all kinds of precious materials and admired by the whole world, was broken into pieces and distributed among the soldiers, as

> well as the other sacred wealth of so great and infinite splendour. When the sacred vases and utensils of unsurpassable art and grace and rare material, and the fine silver, wrought with gold, which enriched the screen of the tribunal and the ambo, of admirable workmanship, and the door and many other ornaments were to be borne away as booty, mules and saddled horses were led to the very sanctuary of the temple. Some of these which were unable to keep their footing on the splendid and slippery pavement, were stabbed when they fell, so that the sacred pavement was polluted with blood and filth. Nay, more! A certain harlot, a sharer in their guilt, a minister of the furies, a servant of demons, a worker of incantations and poisonings, insulting Christ, sat in the patriarch's seat, singing an obscene song and dancing frequently. Nor, indeed, were these crimes committed and others left undone, on the grounds that these were of lesser guilt, the others of greater. But with one consent all the most heinous sins and crimes were committed by all with equal zeal. Could those, who showed so great madness against God Himself, have spared the honourable matrons and maidens or the virgins consecrated to God?'[16]

Stories of this kind no doubt circulated in all Muslim countries, even in such remote areas as Volga Bulgaria. Extending at the end of the 12th century as far as the Yaik (Ural) River, Kol Gali's country maintained close trade and cultural links with Khwarezm, which at that time had attained a position of a relatively great power. Its capital, Urgench, had become one of the most magnificent cities of the Muslim world full of mosques, schools and thriving markets. Travel was comparatively easy and in 1164 the Bolgar sovereign, Khān Salīm had strengthened the fortifications of Kazan and effectively turned what had been a trade and military outpost into a real town. The work of building Kazan was continued by his elder son, Amīr Hājī, but in the Russian chronicles it was always referred to as Saiyin Yurt 'The House of Salim or Sayin'.

The desire for earthly justice, so powerfully expressed in the 'Story of Yusuf' suggests that Kol Gali did not always approve of the way that justice was dispensed. He may have felt alienated from his society, the moral values of which suffered during the time of its prosperity. It is not known whether he travelled at his own free will or whether he was forced to change his place so often because of differences with the powerful people in the courtly or clerical circles, but the bitterness which sometimes shows through his work may well be due to such experiences. The ideals of Muslim unity and harmony also suffered, and the plot of the 'Story of Yusuf', sold into slavery by his brothers, was more than appropriate for the age.

At this time in the Far East, the nomads of Mongolia united under the leadership of Temüchin, who took as his title Chingīz Khān (1162–1227). Having subdued the rebellious tribes, whose name is recorded in Chinese sources as Ta-Ta, the victorious ruler turned his eye to China and the Muslim civilisations of the West. Of the latter, Khwarezm became the first victim of Chingīz's desire for world domination. In 1219 this infant empire fell in a matter of weeks. For Sufis and poets like Kol Gali this was a sign of God's punishment for the earthly pride and transgressions of a decadent society.

Such calamities were a severe threat to international trade and as the southern markets were cut off, Volga-Bulgaria relied more on local outlets, which were constantly challenged by the Russians. In 1218, the Bulgars launched an offensive along the Kama and Vyatka rivers in order to prevent the Russian town of Ustyug usurping their trade with the lands to the north of Volga-Bulgaria. In retaliation the Vladimir-Suzdal army burned down the Bulgar town of Ashly (Oshel) on the right bank of the Volga. Peace was concluded in 1221, but a far greater threat was fast approaching.

Having conquered the main cities of Central Asia such as Bukhara, Samarkand, Urgench and Merv, the Mongol armies launched an attack on the Kipchak Steppe where in 1223 they defeated the combined armies of the local Turks and Russians. In the autumn of the same year the Mongol general, Subedey, attempted to take Volga Bulgaria. This failed as did two further attempts in 1229 and 1232, when the Mongols were repelled by the staunch resistance of the Bulgars and Russians. But this was the last military success of Volga-Bulgaria. In the autumn of 1236 the Mongols captured the city of Bolgar and reduced most of the neighbouring towns to ashes. The last sovereign of independent Volga-Bulgaria, Ilhām Khān, who had successfully organised the resistance of 1223 and 1229 was killed in the final battle with his formidable enemy. Some have suggested that Kol Gali also fell victim to the siege of the city of Bolgar, but his work which had already achieved great popularity was preserved. Although the Volga Bulgars lost their independence, their possessions and their estates to the Mongol invaders they did not lose their religious faith or their culture. Kol Gali died at the height of the Volga Bulgar civilisation, and his work remained a lasting monument to the spirit of its survival.

THE RISE AND FALL OF THE GOLDEN HORDE
(1256–1400)

They brought Suhail up from his prison-vault;
Geldersen held her breath as this was done.
She looked and whirled around her handsome man,
Just like the earth revolving round the sun.

Saif-i Sarai

The quatrain quoted above is taken from the lengthy poem *Suhail and Geldersen* composed by the Golden Horde poet Saif-i Sarai. The 'Book of Yusuf' stands at the end of the Volga-Bulgaria period of Tatar poetry; the works of Saif-i Sarai may be regarded as the climax of the next, much more troubled period of Tatar literary history.

Having conquered and practically destroyed the prosperous Islamic lands of Khwarezm and Persia, having sacked Baghdad and occupied the whole of the Caucasus, in May 1223 Chingīz Khān crushed the unified armies of the Kipchaks and Russians thus opening for himself the way to Europe. Before proceeding, the Mongols first turned to the east and moved through the lands of Volga-Bulgaria. This proved to be a mistake. The Bulgar and Kipchak forces lay in ambush and, as the historian Ibn-al Nasir states, hardly four thousand Mongol warriors escaped alive from the massacre[17]. The Mongol high-command, would not make the same mistake twice.

Chingīz Khān died in 1227 having earlier bequeathed to his son Jochi the vast area of his empire henceforth called the Ulus Jochi which encompassed not only the territories of Central Asia and Siberia and those of the Kipchaks and Volga Bulgars but also all the lands of Rus and those to the west which were still to be conquered. But Jochi was murdered six months before the death of his father and the empire fell into the hands of his son, Batu, who was to head the Golden Horde and play such a prominent part in the conquest of Rus, Hungary and the Balkans.

After their march westwards the Mongol armies stopped on the shores of the Adriatic, where the news of the death of the Great Khan, Ögedei at Karakoram reached Batu Khān in 1242. All the Mongol nobles of royal blood were immediately summoned to the capital, and the question of the succession was regarded as being far more important than any further conquests in the West. The empire had become vast and the balance of Mongol power in the Ulus Jochi needed constant military and political attention. The time of conquest thus ended, and Batu never returned to Mongolia. Having rejected the throne of Karakoram he chose to settle in the region of the Lower Volga from which he ruled his immense domain until his death in 1256.

It has been argued that before founding the new capital of Sarai on the lower reaches of the Volga, Batu established his headquarters in the old Bulgar trading city of Ibrahim-Bryahimov[18]. The troops and horses of Batu's army required the provision of wheat which could be easily supplied from Volga Bulgaria in spite of the destruction the region had suffered during the past conflicts. With this began the period which in Russia is termed 'the Tatar Yoke'.

After their invasion of the region the Mongols and hence their subjects were usually referred to by the name *Tatar*, but there is no really satisfactory explanation as to why this should have been so[19]. Indeed little is known of the Mongols before the twelfth century, though the name in its Chinese form, *Mong-wu*, is attested in documents belonging to the T'ang dynasty (618–907). The various tribes of Mongolia are often referred to as Turko-Mongol, a term which simply means that some of them spoke Turkish while others had Mongolian as their mother tongue. At the time of Chingīz Khān's birth the Tatar tribe seems to have been the most powerful. They obviously incurred the wrath of Chingīz who later in his career set about exterminating them. When the process of extermination was under way, Chingīz's mother actually adopted a Tatar boy whose name is recorded as Shigi-Qutuqu. It has also been suggested that later the term Tatar was used for anyone who had become 'politically' Mongol. It may even be that, because of the former influence of the tribe, Tatar was simply applied to the people as a whole. Indeed the Sung envoy, Chao Hung in 1221 described all Mongols as Tatars, dividing them into 'Black, white and wild'. The common spelling employed in most European languages, *Tartar*, is based on a false comparison with the Latin *Tartarus* – the river of infernal regions, implying 'a people from Hell!' The pun is ascribed by Mathew Paris to Louis IX of France[20] (20).

Among the Kazan Tatars there are many differences of opinion regarding the name, and often bitter arguments about the connections between their own nation and the Tatars of the Golden Horde. Defenders of the theory of purely Bulgar descent argue reasonably enough that their nation was already formed before the onslaught of Chingīz Khān. The eminent Kazan scholar, M. Usmanov, writes as follows:

> 'The ethnogenesis of the Tatar people like that of any large nation which possesses a rich and complex history cannot be ascertained unambiguously. This is because the Middle Volga region . . . was a genuine 'cauldron of nations' in which many ethnic components boiled and blended. Bulgar society was . . . also multi-ethnic. Subdued in 1236 by the Mongol Khans, the Volga-Bulgars lived for two hundred years within the framework of the Golden Horde. The prevalent ethnic component was that of Kipchak-speaking Turkic tribes, which, being dominant in the political and to a certain extent in the cultural sense 'swallowed' the Bulgars and parts of the Finno-Ugric population of the region. For this reason the problem of ethnogenesis cannot be resolved upon a 'whether . . . or' principle; rather more applicable here is the principle of 'and . . . and.'[21]

The opposite argument, by which the very idea of the Kazan Tatars being Tatars in the original sense of the term is strongly denied, has been convincingly put by A. Karimullin:

> 'In Central Asia, India and Persia, where the Mongols stayed in permanent contact with the local people and where they sometimes resided for centuries in much closer contact with the locals than they did in the Middle Volga region, those locals, in spite of frequently being labelled Tatars, did not actually turn into Tatars, but remained Persians, Tajik, Kirghiz, Uzbek, Kazakh etc.'[22]

With the breakdown of the Golden Horde as a single unified state came the establishment of the Kazan, Astrakhan and Crimean Khanates, and from this time it seems that the population of these Khanates began to refer to themselves as Tatars rather than Bulgars. In Kazan, however, people were unhappy about using the term for themselves, regarding it as a derogatory nick-name. According to Sigismund Herberstein, whose eyewitness account of Kazan was written in the 1520s:

> 'If they (the people of Kazan) are called Turks or Tatars they feel most unhappy and take it as abuse. The term "Muslims", on the contrary, pleases them.'[23]

Again the 16th century Tatar poet Muhammedyar, addressing of the one of his literary heroes says:

> 'O you hapless and stupid Tatar!
> You resemble a dog. See your face.
> Diseased and inhuman you are,
> Condemned by the whole Muslim race!

Infidel! Your looks tell the truth.
You are wicked and evil your eyes.
You are lice-ridden, inside and out,
Full of gossip, calumny and lies![24]

The use of the word Tatar as a term of abuse seems to have been well-established during the period of the Golden Horde, and the Russians may have originally adopted it as a synonym for 'bad person' of 'foe'. First it may have been employed only for their Mongol masters, and, after the fall of Kazan, for the whole population of the Kazan Khanate.

Whatever the validity of the various etymologies and proposed explanations of the appellation might be, it is usually held that the Kazan Tatars are basically a Turkic people of Bulgar-Kipchak stock rather than Mongolian. The actual Mongolian component of the nation is probably equal in quantity to that of the Finno Ugric and Slav tribes who had fled to Volga-Bulgaria after Kiev-Rus began enforced baptism of its subjects. These refugees subsequently embraced Islam, scattered themselves among the native Turkic population and adopted their language, which itself became the *lingua franca* of the Golden Horde.

The Mongol nobility, who at first despised 'those decadent Muslims' for their urban rather than nomadic, way of life, soon began to live in towns. From the newly built city of Sarai on the lower Volga to Kazan a chain of towns of varying sizes came into existence, and under the rule of the Golden Horde Khān, Berke (1257–66), Islam became the official religion. The local form of Turkish became the accepted state language and was written in Arabic characters. Literature once more began to flourish, the greatest influences being as elsewhere the Persian works of Rūmī, Sa'di, Hāfiz and others. The common poetic forms were the well-established *qasīda* 'ode' and *ghazal* 'lyric' which are found in all Islamic literatures. The *qasīda*, the major classical Arabic poetic genre, can be formally defined as a lengthy poem with a rhyme scheme AA BA CA etc. most often written in praise of one's lord or patron, lending itself to extravagant descriptions of natural scenery, valour and moral rectitude. The *ghazal*, originally the portion of the *qasīda* which dealt with themes of love and beauty, and hence possessing the same metrical form and rhyme-scheme, was developed as a separate genre by the Persians. Usually a short lyric of seven to ten verses, the *ghazal* became the ideal medium for expressing one's thoughts on almost any subject, human or mystic, though love, and particularly unrequited love, has always been its main subject. Other closely related verse forms, such as the *munajāt* 'prayer, supplication', recited as a religious chant at meetings of Sufi mystics, were also popular among the Tatars of the early period.

The Mongol capital, Sarai, which was described by the Arab geographer, Ibn Battuta, as 'one of the most beautiful cities, full of people, with beautiful bazaars and wide avenues', was also the home of many poets, most of whom are known to us only from their names. One of the earliest pieces of verse which has come down to us from this period is the fairly lengthy poem *Jamjamā Sultān* 'The Skull King' by Hisam Kyatib (Hisām Kātib). Several manuscripts of the work are extant and recent research by Tatar scholars has shown that it was completed around 1375–76 AD in one of the Volga towns. The author's pen-name *Kyatib* 'scribe' probably refers to his profession as a scribe of one of the civic or religious institutions. The story of the poem is a reworking of the old legend of the skull, which once belonged to a proud monarch. This gives the poet plenty of scope to reflect upon the follies of human-kind and the fate awaiting men in the life hereafter.

A similar theme is taken up by the author of the famous *Kisek-bash* 'Severed Head', which also belongs to the Golden Horde period. In the poem, a severed head relates the painful experiences of its erstwhile owner to the Companions of the Holy Prophet. It is finally restored to its owner by 'Alī, who alone has the fortitude to brave the Jinn who had taken its master captive. This poem was especially popular with its Kazan Tatar audience, so much so that Gabdullah Tukai (1886–1913) wrote a satirical version of it applying its well-loved images and ideas to his own world. The fact that Tukai could so freely make use of the medieval original demonstrates his conviction that a modern audience would have no difficulty with the allusions so liberally used in his poem. Indeed, the *Kisek-bash* formed part of the curriculum in Tatar schools as late as the 1920's.

One of the most outstanding poets of the Golden Horde period was Saif-i Sarai (1321–1396), whose verse is contained in two manuscripts now in Leiden[25]. From the pen-name he assumed it is obvious that he had strong links with the capital, Sarai, which at this time was ruled by Uzbek Khān. Research has shown that he was born in the town of Kamyshly, which is probably to be identified with modern Kamyshin in the Volgograd region of Russia. Of himself the poet says:

> *My native town was fairest Kamyshly.*
> *My quest for knowledge brought me to this shore,*
> *And in Sarai I fell prey to the lion.*
> *A poet of Sarai I was, but poor!*

Nothing more is known of his stay in Sarai, but his departure from the city was no doubt due to an outbreak of plague (the forerunner of the Black Death) from which more than 85,000 people died in the Crimea alone. According to the Russian chronicles, 'in the lands of Uzbek Khān the towns and villages were emptied of people' and 'in Sarai, Astrakhan, Urgench and other cities so many died that those left alive could not cope with burying the dead'[26]

To escape the plague and the civil disorder, which marked the general decline of the Golden Horde, Saif-i Sarai fled to Egypt where according to his own writings he stayed from 1380 to 1395. A number of Golden Horde scholars of logic and jurisprudence were already established in Cairo, and, as an outstanding man of letters Saif-i Sarai was welcomed in their midst. A certain Mahmūd Saraī Gulistānī had been appointed as the Chief of the Inshā Dīwān (the office for incoming and outgoing mail) of Sultān Barkuk (1382–99), and it has been suggested that Saif-i Sarai took up employment as a clerk in the office.

While in Cairo, Saif-i Sarai wrote a Turkish version of the *Gulistān* 'The Rose-Garden' of the famous Persian poet, Shaikh Sa'dī. He dedicated his work which was entitled *Gulistān bit-Turkī* to his patron, the Emir Taikhas. The Leiden manuscript in which his 'translation' is preserved also contains verses written by him in answer to other poets including Khwārizmī, and two other Golden Horde writers, Ahmed Khoja of Sarai and 'Abdul Majīd of Crimea, the author of another version of the story of Joseph and Zulaikha[27].

Saif-i Sarai's *Gulistān* is not a literal translation of the Persian text but, composed as the result of what he refers to as 'a scholarly discourse with other men of letters in a fruit-garden amid the flowers', and contains many of his own additions. Frequently departing from the original text he expresses his own personal feelings and political ideas. He often expands the verses, turning four lines into twelve making them more readily accessible to those who spoke Turkish as their mother tongue. The work was completed in 1391. In addition to the *Gulistān*, Saif-i Sarai also composed a number of fine *ghazals* and *qasīdas*, which in form and imagery closely follow their popular Persian counterparts.

Towards the end of his life his world was yet again rocked, this time, by the cruel and bloody invasion of Tīmur ('Tamerlane') who in 1388 sacked and ravaged Urgench, the capital of former Khwarezm, which for generations Bulgar and Golden Horde writers had regarded as the foremost seat of learning. The destruction of Urgench, during which 'the fields were laid bare and human blood ran like water' inspired the longest original work of Saif-i Sarai entitled *Suhail and Geldersen.* These are the names of the two ill-starred lovers whose story unfolds against the background of the calamity, which befell Urgench. Suhail, a warrior, is taken prisoner and is thrown into an underground jail. Geldersen, the daughter of a local ruler, falls in love with him at first sight and organises his escape from the prison. The two lovers flee to the desert, where they suffer from hunger and thirst. While Suhail is away searching for provisions, Geldersen dies of her sufferings, and Suhail, returning and finding her dead, kills himself with his dagger.

Both perished and were buried by the sands that ran;
The desert knows their secret more than any man.

Although Saif-i Sarai states that his story is true, there is little that is original about the plot, which follows that of many similar legends. Saif-i Sarai's version still awaits a satisfactory edition. In other versions Suhail is said to be the son of the Golden Horde Khān, Tokhtamish, and Geldersen the daughter of Tīmur himself. Saif-i Sarai's verse is, however, distinctive and indeed quite beautiful. The tender account of eternal love is the antithesis of the bloody conflicts of the age in which he lived.

Tokhtamish, originally the protégé of Tīmur, was eventually overthrown by the great conqueror who had given him his power. In 1395 the armies of Tīmur advanced as far as Bolgar which was razed to the ground. 'The city of Bolgar which numbered 10,024 houses became nought; only its name remained in the world'[28]. The havoc created by Tīmur's invasion was even greater than the destruction caused by Chingīz and Batu. The entire population of a city would be led out and massacred to the last man. Similar devastation came about when Astrakhan was taken in the winter of 1395–96. The site of the city was abandoned and it was later rebuilt some distance away. The same fate befell Sarai, which was completely burnt and flattened. Tīmur's systematic destruction led to the total impoverishment of the people, the finest professionals and artisans of which were taken captive and sent to Central Asia. The land was laid waste to such an extent that Tīmur's troops themselves almost died of hunger on their return to their homelands that same winter of 1395–96.

Saif-i Sarai died in Cairo in 1396 and with his death the literary and cultural ambience of the Golden Horde period came to an end. The once united country split into a number of separate Khanates, among them that of Kazan, from which time opens another chapter in the history of the Volga Tatars and their verse.

THE KAZAN KHANATE (1436–1552)

> *The joy of death has come at last;*
> *Our happiness has fled away,*
> *And like an eagle it has flown.*
> *We shall not see our cherished day.*[29]

It is possible that Kazan, which is advantageously situated on the left bank of the Volga, was founded as a fortress against southbound Viking pressure as early as the 10th century AD. Later it served as a customs checkpoint for traders on their way to Bolgar the Great from the Finnish north, Russia and the rest of Europe. The importance of Kazan greatly increased when after the fall of Volga Bulgaria, the town inherited the trade of the former state and became a centre for culture. But this did not come about immediately.

The people of Volga Bulgaria, who were periodically forced to flee from constant invasion, plague and drought, when they returned usually chose to settle to the north of their original lands. A small frontier town, known as Bolgar al-Jadīd 'New Bolgar' had already existed for several centuries. In the Turkic languages, the word *kazan* means 'cauldron', and many explanations have been offered for the choice of the word as the name of the city. One of these refers to legend according to which a certain nomad *khān* lost his cauldron in the river, and thus the site of Kazan was named 'the place of the cauldron'. It is also probable that the name of the city is derived from the imperative verbal form *kazan* 'achieve, win over'.

What remained of the old city of Bolgar after Tīmur's attack in 1395 was finally demolished in 1415 by the troops of the Russian prince, Fyodor Pestry, one of the heroes of the Battle of Kulikovo of 1380 at which the Muscovites defeated the Mongol forces. The Golden Horde at this time was already on the brink of collapse, and its *khāns* and their usurpers vied for supremacy while its fate was being decided by the struggle between Tokhtamish and Tīmur.

The Khān of Sarai, Ulug Muhammad, having been driven out of the city by his rivals finally settled in Kazan in 1436 and subsequently made it the capital of the dynasty he founded there. It has also been argued that it was Ulug Muhammad's son, Mahmūd, who founded the dynasty. In any case by 1450 the Kazan Khanate had become a large state occupying the area within the boundaries of Volga Bulgaria from which it inherited its economy and culture. Soon becoming a centre for international trade, Kazan emerged as a powerful economic and political rival of Moscow, which after the collapse of the Golden Horde strove for dominance over all the principalities of Russia. Rivalry often led to wars, and according to the scanty calculations of the contemporary Russian chronicles, more than thirty military campaigns were launched by the Russian principalities and the free city of Novgorod against Volga Bulgaria and the Kazan Khanate, which responded by launching only seven[30].

In 1526, the Austrian Ambassador to the Tsar of Russia, Sigismund Baron von Herberstein, made the following observation on the Kazan Khanate: 'These Tatars are more cultured than others, as they till their fields, live in houses, engage themselves in various trades and seldom go to war'. The Kazan Khanate existed as an independent state till 1552, when it was overpowered by Ivan the Terrible, who after the capture of the city, styled himself 'Tsar', assuming the hereditary title of the Tsars of Kazan.

After the Russian capture of Kazan the city suffered a great loss in terms of both its architecture and culture. In a matter of only a few years the grand Islamic buildings and mosques were replaced by Orthodox Christian churches. The libraries of the Khān's palace and the Great Mosque were burned down and the many manuscripts which they housed were lost for ever, but from the documents and fragments of poetry which survived something of Kazan's medieval culture can be reconstructed.

Like Bolgar and the other important towns of the region, medieval Kazan was distinguished by the oriental style of its architecture. The local nobles constructed two-storey houses for themselves; the skyline of the city was dominated by the Khān's palace, the law-court, a caravanserai, public baths, mausoleums and elegant mosques. These buildings included fine brick and stone vaulted rooms, halls with columns and arcades decorated with frescoes, mosaics and marble inlaid floors. Some eyewitnesses called Kazan 'the capital of the East'. The main mosque of Kazan, the Kol Sharif, named after a religious leader who was himself a distinguished poet and philosopher, was a huge stone edifice with eight lofty minarets.

The most famous building of the present-day Kazan Kremlin is the seven-storey red-brick Suyumbika Tower standing 58 metres high. There are many legends connected with the tower, one of the best known of which is associated with the last Queen of the Khanate. It is said that she threw herself from its summit when the city was stormed by Ivan's army. However romantic the frequently quoted story may be, it is not true. Queen Suyumbika, before the final siege of Kazan, voluntarily let herself become a hostage for peace and was taken to Moscow, where she and her son later died in captivity.

The 'official' version of the origin of the tower is that it was constructed by Russian builders as a military watchtower in the 17th century. Tatar versions, however, attribute it to Bolgar builders and trace its architectural origins back to the pre-Russian period[31].

Several questions support the Tatar claim. Why, for example, should the Russians have erected such an expensive edifice in the 17th century when all national insurgency in the Kazan Khanate had been completely suppressed and the area had long been at peace? If they did, then why build the tower in an obviously Muslim shape, when Russian orthodoxy was ruthlessly directed against Islam? On the other hand, one may well ask why the tower, if it existed at the time of the Russian onslaught, was not destroyed along with the other buildings of the city.

The theory of the early existence of the Suyumbika Tower may perhaps be supported by the following lines of the Kazan poet Muhammedyar, who was apparently alive in 1552.

In the year nine-hundred and forty-eight
On the eighteenth day of the blessed month of Muharram,
At the gate of the Bulgar city of Kazan
Through which many people pass,
By the grave of Muhammad Amīn,
I, poor wretch, live as guardian of that tomb.

Muhammad Amīn, who is regarded as one of the most enlightened rulers of Kazan, ascended the throne of the Khanate in 1487 with the assistance of the Grand Prince of Moscow, Ivan III, who is said to have treated him like an adopted son. His long reign brought an end to the civil disorder and bloody feuds which had continued for 21 years prior to his accession. He was also a poet and benefactor of the arts and in one of his poems *The Calamity* he vividly describes the attack of Tīmur.

> *The world was ruined; Islam lay broken, shattered,*
> *And tears like rivers flowed down every cheek.*
> *Now what will be his answer before Allah*
> *When he is questioned for his evil deeds?*
> *O God! Wouldst Thou reward that slave of Thine*
> *With pains and torture in the life to come!*

Recent excavations around the Suyumbika Tower have revealed the presence of a medieval burial site and one of the tombs is believed to be that of Muhammad Amīn. The poet, Muhammedyar's reference to himself being a guardian of the royal grave may suggest that he actually tended the tomb at the foot of the tower, which he calls 'the gate of the Bulgar city of Kazan'.

To this we can add that while exiled to Moscow, Muhammad Amīn witnessed the building of the Kremlin by the Italian architect, Aristotle Fioravanti of Bologna. It is quite possible that he persuaded his protector to send an Italian architect to Kazan in order to build a tower commemorating his alliance with Moscow. Indeed certain architectural features of the Suyumbika Tower resemble those of the Calvaria San Stefano and the Piazza Maggiore towers of Bologna, and the size of bricks tallies with the standard which was introduced into Moscow by Fioravanti. The Russian standard adopted a hundred years later differs essentially from Fioravanti's standard, and this is further evidence against the theory that the tower was built by Russians in the 17th century.

Little else is known of the life of the poet Muhammadyar, whose major surviving works, *Tuhfaye Mardan (Tuhfa-i-Mardān)* 'The Gift to Young Men' (1539) and *Nure Sodur (Nūr-i Sudūr)* 'The Light of Breasts' (1542) have much in common with the verse ascribed to Hoja Ahmed Yasavī and are greatly influenced by Naqshbandi Sufi teachings which had become widespread in Volga-Bulgaria and the Kazan Khanate. Both works deal with ethical and moral issues and are divided into several chapters, each dealing with a particular virtue such as justice, patience, generosity and so forth. Like all Sufis, Muhammadyar preferred an independent existence away from the comfort and intrigues of the court. He stands out as one of the foremost poets of the Kazan Khanate and like his predecessors, Kol Gali and Saif-i Sarai makes many interesting reflections on the day-to-day life of the city and the views and morals of his contemporaries.

Other poets who flourished in Kazan at this period are known only from their names which are mentioned in other sources or from stray fragments of their verse which have been preserved by chance. Among them are Garifbek (ʿĀrif Beg) and the Kipchak writer Asar Kaighi. Ömmi Kamal is mentioned in the Ottoman archives and it is thought that he may have been a wandering dervish of the Shaikh Bahavetdin school[32]. We know that he died in 1475. His poems are composed in Seljuk Turkish, but are said to contain elements of Tatar-Kipchak. He talks of the former territories of the Golden Horde, including Kazan and the Crimea as 'alien lands', but the small portion of his verse which has come down to us has always fascinated and indeed influenced Kazan Tatar poets even down to the 20th century. Ömmi Kamal's rich descriptions of nature and its beauty are among the first of their kind to be attested from the time of the Kazan Khanate:

> And every creature praises Allah in its way;
> Beasts roam the valleys; birds regale the air with song.
> Amid the flowers the nightingale sang of his love;
> Upon the rose he perched; his lay was sad and long.
>
> So hard he strove his praise and wonderment to show,
> In ecstasy he fell down to the grass below.

Of Kol Sharif, who gave his name to the Jāmi' Mosque of Kazan more is known because of his position as a diplomat and he is therefore mentioned in the Russian chronicles. His father was Sayyid Mansūr, a prominent religious figure who in 1546 stood up against the unjust rule of the Moscow protégé, Shāh 'Alī. Sayyids, who claim to be descendants of the Holy Prophet, always occupied leading positions in the hierarchy of the Khanate, and Kol Sharif, after his father's death became the leader of the local Muslims in his place. He is said to have perished in the final battle for Kazan when the Muscovite army was met with the resistance of a handful of defenders at the Kol Sharif Mosque. As we have seen, most of the city's archives and manuscripts were lost in the fire, which followed the Russian attack, but a few of Kol Sharif's poems survived. These were published in 1997 in the form of a small booklet in Kazan, and comprise eight *ghazals* and one mystic *qissa*. His verse is typical of Sufi composition known from elsewhere, expressing a strong sense of spiritual morality:

*My soul! Do not yield to the world.
This world is for ever constrained;
And all those who live in this world
To the goblet of death are chained.*

*Do not fancy that you will remain
In this world for long; for its fire
Is kindled and blazes anew
With the flames that will burn your pyre.*

The annexation of the Kazan Khanate by Ivan the Terrible was in many ways more terrible and destructive than the attack of Tīmur. Not only were the Tatars under foreign domination, but they were forbidden from entering their own cities under pain of death. The survivors were ordered to settle thirty miles away from any large town, and for that reason their traditional culture was effectively banished to the countryside. From that time onwards all major poets were born and educated in the villages, which themselves became seats of learning. Since Islam had become a persecuted faith, from the late 16th century well into the 18th such activities had to be carried on in a clandestine fashion. Mosques were destroyed and Orthodox Christian churches were built on their sites. After several decades, when trade in Kazan had declined, the Tatars were allowed to reside on the outskirts of their former illustrious capital in the Old and New Tatar settlements which now form a part of the city of Kazan. Suppression of culture and religion resulted in the fact that out of some six million Tatars only a quarter now remain in the territory of their original homeland. The rest were forced to leave for places where they were free to profess their faith. With the rapid expansion of the Russian Empire, fewer and fewer such places remained available for them on the Volga or in the Urals. Thus colonies of Tatars are now to be found as far away as China and Japan.

The name 'Kazan Khanate' designating the conquered region was still in use up to the beginning of the reign of Peter the Great (1672–1725). In spite of its alienation, Tatar culture was not only in close contact with that of Russian Orthodoxy, but even influenced it. There is little evidence of racial enmity between Slav and Tatar at this time. In 1593, Archbishop Germogen, whose task it was to baptise the local Tatar population, wrote in one of his letters: 'Many former Russian captives and free men live with the Tatars, the Cheremis and the Chuvash, eat and drink with them from the same bowl, and marry their girls'[33]. This letter and others similar to it prompted the order for all the remaining mosques and religious schools of the Kazan Khanate to be finally destroyed.

The fate of the last poet of the Kazan Khanate, Mevla Koly, (Maulā Kolī) is in many ways indicative of what was happening to Tatar culture and literature throughout the 17th century. His real name was Bairamgali Koliev and because of his mystic background he was popularly called Bimka Sufi. He was born in the village of Chity to a family of so-called 'Cossack Tatars', people who served the Russian administration of the region but who were otherwise allowed to remain faithful to their national culture.

Mevla Koly was educated in Kazan in the school of a certain Mullah Mamai on the outskirts of the city. According to contemporary Russian archives, it was he who led the Tatars of various districts when in 1678 they were given permission to settle near the ruins of the ancient Bulgar city, Bilyar. In 1699, however, this Tatar settlement was replaced by an orthodox settlement and its inhabitants were ordered to re-settle in the village of Old Ishtiryak on the banks of the Sheshma river. The descendants of Mevla Koly have lived in that region ever since.

Mevla Koly's poems strongly reflect the Sufi traditions dating back to the age of Ahmed Yasavī, at the same time displaying and making use of local motifs and images which can be found in the verse of Kol Gali and earlier folk songs. He, like many Turkish poets, calls his poems 'hikmet', the Arabic word for 'wisdom'. The *hikmet*, a Turkish quatrain of seven or eleven syllables usually composed on the subject of the miracles of the Prophet, with pronouncements on the vanity of the world and the virtues of the ascetic life, go back to the age of Ahmed Yasavī[34]. In the *divan* dedicated to his teacher, Mullah Mamai, Mevla Koly writes:

> Dear friends! This *hikmet* was written
> In the year 1088 after the Hijra,
> In the region near the city of Bolgar
> By the sinner and tormentor, Maula Koly.

According to Mevla Koly, his master, Mamai, was also a poet, and at that time poets usually came from a religious background. Until the late 18th century, the Kazan Tatars had no official clergy and the maintenance and development of Islam was largely in the hands of laymen like Mevla Koly himself. The title *mullāh* or *maulā* simply meant 'a learned person' who in the big villages would teach not only basic religion but also such subjects as arithmetic and calligraphy.

With the abolition of the name 'Kazan Khanate' at the start of the reign of Peter the Great, Islamic culture was completely confined to the villages, which remained out of the range of the imperial gaze. The former traditions of urban life, however, still remained in people's memory, and in spite of all the tribulations it was forced to endure, Tatar culture soon adapted itself to its orphan status in its own motherland.

TATAR POETRY OF THE RUSSIAN EMPIRE
(18th–19th Centuries)

I

Let them crowd in the streets: let them wander and stray
Not even the Russians will scare me away.
Gabdeljabbar Kandaly

The verse quoted above is by the Tatar poet Gabeljabbar ('Abdul Jabbār) Kandaly who lived in the first part of the 19th century. The lines are intended as a kind of joke and contain a form of the Russian word for street *ulitsa*: *ulistan* 'along the street' which is rhymed with the Tatar word *urystan* 'of a Russian'. Even in his day the employment of Russian words in everyday speech was still considered amusing. During the century after him, the phenomenon became commonplace, and, sad as it may seem, the vast majority of urban Tatars could no longer speak their mother tongue in its pure and correct form. Tatar was removed from the normal school curriculum and regarded by most as being of little importance. During the 18th century representatives of Tatar culture made a great effort to persuade their people that an adequate knowledge of Russian was essential for further national development, but their struggle to convince their fellow countrymen was hard and long. The unwillingness to learn Russian no doubt stems from the policy of enforced baptism which was strongly countered by the spiritual forbearance and conservatism of the mass of the Tatar population.

It is well known that the policies of Peter the Great brought much suffering to the peoples of his ever increasing empire, and serfdom meant that the majority of Russian peasants were treated no better than chattels. The Tatars of the former Kazan Khanate, however, were in some ways more fortunate in as much as the notorious *krepostnoe pravo*, the right of the aristocracy to keep serfs, was never imposed upon them. The Khanate, for which a special Ministry for Kazan had been set up in Moscow, was regarded simply as another province of the Russian Empire. A revolt against the abolition of the country's name was easily put down in 1708 and Kazan was re-captured. In 1713 the Muslim Cossack Tatars lost their privileges and the following decree, the *Kazansky Prykaz*, was issued by Peter the Great:

> 'The Great Tsar orders all unbelievers of the Muhammadan creed in the provinces of Kazan and Azov, who have lands and estates, house serfs and employees of the Christian faith, to receive baptism within six months . . . Should they not become Christian within six months, then all those lands and estates with their workers and peasants shall be taken away and confiscated to the benefit of the Great Tsar.'

These measures, however, did not always meet with the success, which was expected. The inhabitants of converted villages would often return to their original faith as soon as the pressure was lifted. Large numbers of Muslim Tatars became nomadic and tried to settle in places far from the eyes of the authorities. In this way Tatar centres of education were established in the Urals, Orenburg and Siberia and as far away as present-day Kazakhstan, Uzbekistan and Kirgizstan. The notorious 'Office for the Affairs of the Newly Baptised' in 1742 was under the direction of Archbishop Luka Konashevich and during his time the policies of compulsory conversion were enforced with unprecedented fervour. Out of 546 mosques, 418 were demolished in the Kazan district alone and the inhabitants of whole villages were baptised *en masse* at gunpoint, but after the Archbishop's transfer in 1755 the labour of erecting new mosques began afresh.

Repression, which resulted in the gross impoverishment of the Tatar people, also took other forms. The ideologist, Ivan Pososhkov, advised that Tatar children should be removed from their families and forbidden from speaking their mother-tongue. Only then, he argued, would the Tatars turn into 'true Christians'. During the Pugachev uprising, Kazan was captured by the rebels in 1774 and after its recapture by the government forces harsh reprisals were taken on its Tatar population. These excesses, however, were alleviated when in 1784 Catherine the Great changed the most unpopular policies of her predecessor.

The Empress visited Kazan herself and ordered the construction of a new mosque. She also denounced the ordinance, which prevented the Tatars from settling in a 30-mile radius from Kazan, but since these areas were now inhabited by Russian settlers, her decree was no more than a palliative. Nevertheless, her decree of 1788 allowed Tatars to profess their own faith and restrictions on trade were partly lifted.

Freedom to profess Islam resulted in a recrudescence of educational activity and large schools once more began to flourish in the territory of former Volga-Bulgaria and other areas where the Kazan Tatars had settled during the age of persecution. Traditional Islamic places of learning, the *madrasas*, re-appeared in Kazan, Ish-Bobinsk, Ufa, Troitsk and the Tatar settlement of Kargala near Orenburg. Once more scholarly pursuits and composition of Tatar verse began to blossom.

Among the scholars and teachers of the Kargala settlements was Gabdessalam ('Abdussalām) Urai Ugly (c.1700–1762), who was also a renowned poet. During the war between Russia and Prussia which took place between 1757 and 1763, Urai Ugly was recruited into the Russian army as a *mullah*, the experiences of which he described in his poems. He founded a veritable poetic dynasty. His son Abelmanikh Kargaly was also a famous poet, and during the 18th century we come across the names of Sagdetdin Gabdelmajid (Sa'datdīn 'Abdulmajīd) Ugly, Nigmatullah (Ni'matullāh) Bashīr Ugly and others. These writers of the so-called 'New Age of Tatar Poetry' tried to bring a new meaning to the archaic words and images found in the medieval verse of the Kazan Khanate, and the language of their poems was brought much closer to that of everyday speech.

The most significant poet of the 18th century was Gabderrahim ('Abdurrahīm) Utyz Imyani, who was born in 1754 in the village of Yanga Qadi, the former Yanga Utyz Imyan 'The New Thirty Oaks'. He received his basic education from a *mullah* in his own village and then attended *madrasas* in the neighbouring area. Having moved to Kargala where he acquired further education, he left with his family for Central Asia. In Bukhara he became a teacher, then ever in search of knowledge travelled to Samarkand, Herat and Kabul before returning to Bukhara in 1798.

The career of Utyz Imyani is in many ways typical of that of many of his contemporaries. His thirst for knowledge and education drove him along his path during the darkest period of his people's history; he died when Tatar culture was once more in the process of its revival. The historian of Kazan, Professor Karl Fuks, observed in 1844: 'No doubt, every visitor to Kazan will be surprised to find among the Kazan Tatars people who are even more educated than Europeans . . . A Tatar who does not know how to read and write is held in contempt by his fellows and is not respected as a citizen. . . . This nation which has been subjugated for two hundred years and is now scattered amongst the Russians, has been able to preserve its customs, morals and pride so amazingly, as though it had lived separately.'[35]

The University was opened in Kazan in 1804, and this great institution has contributed much to the cultural and scientific life of modern Russia. Its press, which was opened in 1809, was able to function as a profit-making enterprise solely due to the great demand by the Kazan Tatars for books of a religious and cultural nature. The first Tatar press was established with the permission of Tsar Pavel I at the very beginning of the 19th century by G. Burashev, and continued to publish Tatar books until 1829 when it merged with that of Kazan University. In 1845, however, the production of Tatar books in all the Kazan presses was forbidden by royal ordinance. This ordinance was subsequently revoked and in the second half of the 19th century in some years the overall print-run of Tatar books reached some two million copies. In this respect the Kazan Tatars were behind only the Poles, Latvians, Germans, Jews and Estonians of the Russian Empire[36].

There were, of course, always many problems. The publishing of Tatar newspapers was not allowed until 1905. Before this all that existed was an annual calendar prepared from 1871–1897 by the modernist reformer Qayum Nasyri. He was a scholar of encyclopaedic knowledge and it is largely to him that we owe the creation of a modern Tatar literary language based on the spoken dialect of Kazan. His school, which was founded in order to teach Tatar children Russian and secular subjects such as history, geography and arithmetic, earned him the opprobrium of his less educated fellow countrymen who regarded his methods as nothing short of heresy. His work on Russian grammar led him to write on Tatar linguistics, and in his Tatar grammar, he wrote:

> *'While in the process of teaching the Russian language, I sharply felt the necessity of a book which would expound the rules of the Tatar tongue.'*

His work led to the first Explanatory Dictionary of Tatar, entitled *Lughati Tatari*, and the establishment of rules of orthography set out in his *Qavagyide Kitabat (Qavāʿid-i Kitābat)* These books played a vital role in removing from the language many archaic and foreign words, especially those of Ottoman Turkish and Arabic. His great efforts therefore led to the creation of purer Tatar literary style. The poems of Utyz Imyani and his contemporaries, Tajetdin (Tājuddīn) Yalchigol (1786–1839) and Abelmanikh Kargaly still preserved many features of medieval Turkish. The poems of writers of a slightly later period such as Yakov Emelyanov and Gabdeljabbar ('Abduljabbār) Kandaly (1797–1860) were composed in a new poetic diction which was much closer to the spoken language of the day.

The clarity and 'purity' of the language of these two poets can be ascribed to two very different reasons. Yakov Emelyanov was a newly baptised Tatar Christian and became a priest of the Orthodox Church. Being Christians, people like him were cut off from the mainstream of Tatar Muslim culture. At the same time, being Tatars, they were not fully accepted by the orthodox Russians. As a result, the closed existence of the Tatar orthodox communities produced a culture in which the most ancient arts and customs of the Tatars were preserved. For this reason their language is one of the 'purest' of all the Tatar dialects with far less of its vocabulary imported from Russian. The poems of the Christian poet, Garai Rahim (Grigory Vasilyev) are an excellent illustration of this phenomena.

Gabdeljabbar Kandaly on the other hand was born to a family of *mullahs* in 1797 in the village of Old Kandal in the Samara province where his grandparents had settled. Having received, as was customary, his initial education from his father he visited many of the Tatar *madrasas* in places between the Volga and the Urals. Being of an impulsive character and possessing great wit and charm, he instinctively rebelled against everything, which he considered had outlived its usefulness. Because of arguments with his teachers and fellow students he never stayed in any school for long. Many of his satirical poems are written against the pomposity of Tatar 'holy men', and he became famous for his ready improvisations. He returned to his native village in 1824 and took over his father's duties as local *mullah*. In order to qualify for his new function he was first obliged to sit examinations in the newly established Muslim Spiritual Board at Ufa.

His life was always complicated by his continuous disagreements with the rich locals and his expansive behaviour earned him the reputation of being a troublemaker. These activities often became the focus of investigations by both the spiritual and state authorities. He also acquired friends, one of whom offered him the position of Imam in the new mosque, which he had constructed in the village.

He was called upon to perform other duties and for some obscure reason spent some time in jail.

Kandaly, the first *enfant terrible* of Tatar poetry, was known not only for his clever and bitter satire, but also for his beautiful and expressive love poems such as Sahibjamal (Sāhibjamāl), which rank among the best in Tatar literature. He died penniless, broken-hearted and ridiculed by the ignorant in 1860.

The life and deeds of Kandaly should be looked upon against the background of a great spiritual change already under way among the Tatars in his own lifetime. The freedom of conscience granted by the Tsarist authorities brought about a much-needed educational reform based upon the reformist movements of religious revival of Islam. Such religious thinkers as Gabdennasyr ('Abdunnāsir) Kursavi (1783–1830) who was sentenced to death for his freethinking by the Emir of Bukhara, was only one of those who dedicated their lives to the spiritual revival of their nation along with other Muslim nations of the Russian Empire. Having escaped death for alleged heresy, Kursavi returned to the Kazan province and became a teacher in the village of Kursa. In a very short time his fame as a religious philosopher earned him many supporters and even more enemies who complained against him to the Spiritual Board of Muslims in Ufa. Kursavi, with his strong and passionate character, was in his spiritual struggle akin to Kandaly. Kursavi's life would most probably have ended in jail or exile, but he died in Istanbul-Constantinople on his way to the Holy Places of Islam, being only 37 years of age.

In the first quarter of the 19th century we meet the first Tatar women poets. It may be argued that their contribution was not very large, but their very existence shows that Tatar spiritual life, after centuries of male-dominated scholasticism and mystical pursuits, had reached a turning point. These women poets came mostly from a religious background and received their primary education in local girls' schools. The lives of the most notable, such as Galimatelbarat Buktimirova, Hanifa Gismatullina, Galima Rahmatullina and Gaziza Samitova followed much the same pattern. Being daughters of *mullahs* or *madrasa*-teachers they furthered their education through their own efforts and finally became teachers themselves.

G. Buktimirova (1876–1906) learned Russian, Arabic, arithmetic and geography by herself and made a study of both Russian and Oriental literature before becoming a published poet. She married and became a teacher in the local girls' school which she opened and sustained at her own expense. She also wrote a number of educational books, which were received warmly not only by the young women of her generation but also by men, especially those who were themselves Tatar poets and scholars.

In 1902, another outstanding women, Habira Nasyri, the niece of the famous Qayum Nasyri, published her Dictionary of the Arabic, Persian and Turkish Languages.

The verse of Tatar women always laid stress on the value of education and enlightenment, which was perceived as essentially Islamic. The slogan of the day was that of the Holy Prophet: 'O Allah, may Thou multiply my knowledge'. The efforts of people like Qayum Nasyri were followed up and multiplied, and eventually in 1883 in Bakhchisarai, the former capital of the Crimean Khanate, a local businessman, Ismail Gasprinsky fulfilled his long-standing ambition of publishing the very first Muslim newspaper of the Russian Empire. He was also the first one to organise a poetry reading in Kazan, which took place in 1882. In his memoirs he writes:

> *'In 1882, during my stay in Kazan, I wanted to organise a literary event for the Tatars. I obtained permission for this with great effort; the announcements were stuck all over the Tatar quarters of Kazan; a spacious hall in a first-class hotel was hired for the purpose . . . After 9 o'clock in the evening I waited for another two hours, but there were still only three people in the audience. But they were not from Kazan. One was Allah-Yar Bey of the Caucasus; the other two were the brothers Shakir and Zakir Rameev, the future publishers of the Vakit newspaper of Orenburg.'*

The silver age of Tatar literature had dawned, but as yet no-one seemed to be aware of it!

II

> *Sometimes in melancholy I repose*
> *Listening to the stillness of the universe.*
> *A voice resounds in my ears*
>   *I say:*
>   *— What is it?*
>   *— Whence does it come?*
>   *In the place of a response*
>   *Water purls,*
>   *Ivies rustle in the wind.*
>
>   Derdmend

Until 1905, the *Tardzhiman* (*Tarjumān*) newspaper of Gasprinsky was the only organ to publish essays in Tatar on history, philosophy and education and to include original Tatar poetry and verse translations. The Rameev brothers, who had attended Gasprinsky's 'literary event', possessed gold mines in the Urals, and soon acquired vast wealth. Zakir Rameev, one of the most refined Tatar poets of the time actually named his mines after the famous Persian poets, Firdausi and Sa'dī. Their wealth enabled them to launch *Vakit* (*vaqt* 'time'), the first truly Volga-Tatar newspaper in 1906 and two years later the literary magazine, *Shūra* ('council'). Such enterprises were facilitated by the liberal outcome of the Russian Revolution of 1905 and from then until 1917 dozens of Tatar newspapers and magazines saw the light of day.

The tragic figure of Zakir Rameev (1859–1921), who wrote under the pen-name of Derdmend (*Dardmand*) 'The Sad One', even though his work consists of only one small booklet, is of major importance in the development of modern Tatar verse. As a young man he became convinced that a poet should free himself from the demands of everyday life. This of course was far easier for him than for others since he was a very wealthy man. He and his elder brother Shakir were great benefactors of charitable enterprises in the field of Tatar education and publishing. Far from receiving income from their publishing activities, they usually ran them at a considerable loss, because *Vakit* and *Shūra* were printed at double the official print-run and more often than not distributed free of charge. Within less than a decade of their embarking on their enterprise they were overtaken by the Revolution of 1917 which stifled and destroyed all their hopes and aspirations. As a sensitive and far-seeing poet Derdmend had premonitions of things to come and expressed his disappointment in verses, which are considered to be some of the most touching ever written in the language.

> *Summer has gone*
> *The snow and the rain of autumn sets in;*
> *Ice begins to cover the heart of the blue lagoon.*
> *The flower has withered;*
> *On its stem remains a thorn*
> *Ah, nightingale!*
> *For you only the thorn is so dejected.*

Typically Derdmend takes one image or sensation for his poem, drawn from figures employed in the Tatar and Persian verse of earlier ages. Most of his poems are short, but always exhibit great depth and intensity with a vision which often seems to amount to a prophecy. Such a poem is 'The Ship' in which he foresaw the brief period of Russian liberalism leading to the abyss of Communist dictatorship:

> *The sea roars . . .*
> *The strong wind blows . . .*
> *In full sail the ship goes forth*
> *Day and night*
> *She wanders and roams*
> *Looking for unknown shores . . .*
> *Winds abate*
> *Waves abound*
> *In which direction is our nation hauled?*
> *Which abyss,*
> *Which deadly paths*
> *Beckon to us, demanding our soul?*

Derdmend was born in the village of Jirgan in the southern Urals, and received his education in an Istanbul *madrasa*. During his life his travels took him to Germany, France and Italy, and his sons and daughters were educated in various colleges in other parts of Europe. In 1917 he could easily have left Russia but, even after losing his gold mines and other properties in the programme of nationalisation which took place after the Revolution, he elected to stay. He lost everything and died in 1921 from penury and hunger in the small town of Orsk.

Before his death he witnessed the flooding of the Ural River, and the terrible picture of corpses floating with the raging current under the windows of Derdmend's house is portrayed in the poems of his son, Yangfar. Because Derdmend had served, albeit reluctantly, in the Red Army, he was spared execution which was the fate of many former rich industrialists. Yangfar, however, in spite of being a veteran of the Civil War of 1918–20 was forced to go into hiding in a village of the Chelyabinsk province of the Urals. The shadow of his father's 'capitalist' past haunted him throughout his life and he was never allowed to publish his verse. The editor of the newspaper to which he first sent his poems warned him to lie low in his village of Altyntash without revealing his descent.

The fate of Yangfar, though bad enough, was less tragic than that of many other young Tatar poets, who, having embarked on their literary career just before 1917, soon fell victim to the suffocating atmosphere of the early Soviet years. Many, like the romantic revolutionary, Sagit Rameev (no relation of Derdmend) died prematurely or were executed for advocating their ideas of national revival. Gabdulla Tukai, who is now considered to be one of the finest Tatar poets of the period, had already died of tuberculosis in 1913 at the age of 26, thus escaping what might have befallen him after the Revolution.

The poetry of Tukai has a special place in the hearts of the Tatars who see his work as the pinnacle of their long literary tradition. As is often the case with writers of genius his work only became fully appreciated after his untimely death. His tragic life is now often viewed as a metaphor for the history of his nation. Born in 1886, he was orphaned at the age of three, and never had a real home of his own. At the end of his life he rented a small room in a hotel where he could entertain his friends.

Tukai was like many of his contemporaries educated in the local *madrasa* in the village of Kurlai, which he mentions with affection in his beautifully lyrical poem, *Shuraleh*. Here the tale of the Tatar forest demon provides him with the opportunity to offer rich descriptions of the countryside he enjoyed and loved. He furthered his education in the town of Uralsk where he studied until 1905. Finding employment as a typographer for the journals *Fiker* (*fikr* 'Thought') and *Al-'Asr al Jadīd* ('The New Age') he became a regular contributor to both magazines. Famous for his hospitality offered to his friends, some of whom were always ready to take advantage, he remained poor, but his independent character would not allow him to accept Derdmend's invitation to him to join the staff of *Shūra* and *Vakit*, which were being published from Orenburg. He suspected the offer merely to be charity from a fellow poet.

Tukai's work has many of the characteristics of the verse of G. Kandaly. We find the same satirical approach to ignorance and dogmatism, and the same search for love of which he ever remained deprived. He never married, choosing to devote his time to his writing. Within just seven years he produced five volumes of truly excellent poetry which must be regarded as a great achievement for someone living in such adverse conditions.

At the start of his career, Tukai was deeply influenced by Islamic mysticism, but he soon took up the cause of liberal national thought, and tried to reform the approach of the Tartars to the outside world. To this end he wrote his famous parody of the *Book of Kisek-bash*, the medieval Tatar tale of the 'Severed Head'. Tukai's modernised version, which contains witty attacks on dogmatic holy-men and rich fools, is firmly set in the Kazan of his own day; the contemporary circus wrestler, Karakhmet, is substituted for 'Alī, and the conveyance which is used for transporting the hero of the story to the abode of the 'dev', is a speeding tram!.

Like other poets of his time, Tukai abandoned the literary language which was replete with words taken from Arabic, Persian and classical Turkish, and moulded a style which was closer and more faithful to contemporary Tatar idiom. In the use of this fresh and vigorous form of the language he had few rivals. Indeed many of his short poems became what are now regarded as folk songs, one of the most popular being *Mother Tongue*.

My mother tongue! Fair tongue of mine!
My father's and my mother's speech;
Through you so much I hear and learn;
So many people can I reach.

Beside my cradle in your lilt
My mother sang a lullaby;
My grandmother would tell me tales
As evening's dusk came creeping by.

My mother tongue! Your kind support
Has helped my life to run its course;
And since my childhood you have borne
My hopes, my joys and my remorse.

My mother tongue! In you I prayed,
Beseeching God to save my soul.
Forgiveness for my parents too
I sought through you. You made me whole.

Tukai never set out to idealise his people, and though a passionate believer in their national aspirations, he saw no reason to employ sentimental flattery. The directness, forbearance and gentle humour which stand out in his work, with some justification, earned him his unofficial title of *Tugry Tukai* – 'The Truthful Tukai'.

After the world-wide celebration in 1983 of the 800th anniversary of Kol Gali, the writer of the first substantial work of Tatar literature, Gabdulla Tukai's centenary (which of course occurred three years later) was also marked by UNESCO, thus giving both poets both national and world recognition. We must, of course, be careful not to exaggerate the importance of Tukai in terms of world literature, but it is a tribute to the value of his poetic work that almost alone he received the attention of scholars and critics from outside the narrow confines of his own land. His German biographer, Michael Friedrich, wrote in the concluding part of his study:

> 'This Tatar youth from the tiny village, Uchile, which stands in the forests around Kazan, became a poet of world-standing, and forms part of the cultural history of all mankind.'[37]

THE LAKE OF SWANS

But all this is unclear. I will forget:
The movement of the shadows,
The sweet-briar, the lindens,
The slow creaks of the wet bench,
The round edges of the clouds,
The pages illuminated by rays —
But not the poems on civil themes,
Not the poems of civil despair[38].

Kazan is now a large centre for industry and education populated by more than 1,300,000 people of both Tatar and Russian origin. Yet to the present day in its surrounding areas its ancient pine forests remain, in the midst of which in winter and summer gleaming lakes preserve their serene beauty and natural tranquillity. One of these, which has long been a popular recreation spot for the citizens of Kazan is known in Tatar as *Akkosh Kule* and in Russian as *Lebyazhe*, 'The Lake of Swans'. Not everyone who passes the beauty spot, which is situated on the main highway leading from Kazan to Moscow, will know that not far from the lake in a wide forest clearing is hidden a modest settlement of cottages. During the Stalinist period these were hired out at a nominal rent to local authors, poets, critics and playwrights. To occupy or share one of these dwellings was a sign of official recognition, but the comfort of such an existence was bought at a price. Writers were by no means allowed to follow their own inclinations and soon found that certain themes were prohibited. The teaching of the Tatar language was virtually abolished during the 1950's as something 'archaic'; those who studied at the only Tatar school in the city could barely hope to further their education at the university. The *dachas*, however, for all the restrictions imposed by the authorities, still provided the opportunity for younger writers to meet renowned and admired authors and to show each other their literary endeavours and experiments.

As the political situation eased, poets who had been banished to labour camps began to return, and one of the first to take up residence was Hasan Tufan whose powerful Tatar verse has since earned him great respect. Others who took up residence in or frequently visited the complex were Sibgat Hakim, Ravil Faizullin, Renat Haris, Robert Ahmetjanov, Zulfat, Mudarris Aglyamov, Razil Valeev and Fannur Safin, whose names are instantly recognised by all Tatars. Shaukat Galiev and Enver Davydov, as many others, also gained recognition outside the confines of the Tatar ASSR, which in turn would often host literary festivals for writers and poets from every part of the USSR. During these events the names of the Tatar poets of the 1930's, especially the talented Hadi Taktash, would be mentioned with respect and admiration. The verse of Musa Jalil, whose death in the Nazi Moabit prison earned him recognition as a Hero of the Soviet Union, was translated into many of the major languages of the world. He is remembered as the 'last martyr of Tatar poetry'!

Until the 1970's it was of course perilous to argue with the 'official' version of Tatar history which had been rewritten according to the Marxist axioms of the Stalinist era. Here the capture of Kazan by Ivan the Terrible in 1552 and the effects of the 1917 Revolution were proclaimed as the happiest moments of Kazan Tatar history, and even the earliest Tatar works had to be viewed and studied (if studied at all) in the framework of official historiography. In 1944 the Tatar Research Institute for Language, Literature and History was condemned outright by the regional Communist Party on the grounds that after 'thorough investigation' its activities were 'injurious to the health of society'. 'Damaging' and 'pro-religious' works by the most popular poets like Mevla Koly, Utyz Imyani and Kandaly were proscribed and taken out of the school curriculum.

The designation of the Tatars as a 'feudal nation', which was required to take a giant leap from the abyss of its medieval darkness to the shining heights of Socialism, had important consequences. The usefulness of the Arabic alphabet in which the language had been written for centuries was discounted. Twice in two decades, in 1920 and 1939, the Kazan Tatars were obliged to change their script, first to Roman and then to a modified form of Cyrillic. This, of course, rendered all that had been published prior to the reforms unusable.

A similar fate befell many other peoples of the Soviet Union, but many of them were at least allowed to retain their folklore and national epics. The Kazan Tatars were not so fortunate and by the same edict of 1944 the Tatar version of the epic poem of *Edighey* was totally banned and almost lost completely. The *Edighey*, an anonymous composition belonging to the period of the Golden Horde, was probably compiled in the late 14th century. In its lines the author laments the disunity and imminent disintegration of the Horde. The poem is also found in Kazakh, Nogai, Kirgiz and other Turkic languages, but it was the Kazan Tatar version that was singled out for criticism and final proscription. The Bureau's written condemnation of the epic and hence of the work of the Tatar institute in general is tedious and predictable and there is no need to quote it in full here. Suffice it to say that in the document the phrases 'against the people', 'nationalist sentiments', 'lack of progressive significance', 'aggrandisement of the Golden Horde' and 'serious mistakes' feature prominently.

It was inevitable that the Tatar writers of the twentieth century who through their education became fully conversant with Russian should also have been influenced by its literature. Because of shared experiences the works of all Soviet authors exhibit many common themes. It is always vain to make direct comparisons, but it would be fair to say that the war poems of Musa Jalil and Sibgat Hakim, the rich descriptions of nature by Ildar Yuzeev and Garai Rahim, and the vague nostalgia expressed in the verse of Renat Haris and Ravil Faizullin are in every way equal to the contributions made by both Russian and non-Russian poets of the Soviet and post-Soviet eras.

Although it is impossible to predict what the future of the Tatar language and its literature might be, there is every reason for optimism. As always economic factors present the greatest obstacles, and, as in most countries of the world, poets can rarely make a living from their writing, but times have changed and in the present atmosphere of freedom they are at least able to say what they wish and express themselves how they wish. As far as language is concerned, there are yet again proposals to change the alphabet and return to the Roman script within the next ten years. By some this new plan is greeted with trepidation and the question might be asked whether it is not too much for a people to lose its literary heritage four times in one century!

Throughout their chequered history the Tatars have given much from which others can profit and derive pleasure. From the earliest times their land has been ravaged by invaders; the people have often been forced into exile; the language has been relegated to the status of some insignificant tongue fit only for the village *madrasa*. It is indeed surprising that it survived at all. By the efforts of writers and scholars who have usually worked in the most miserable and uninspiring circumstances the literature and its traditions have remained alive and in the future are likely to thrive. Much work, of course, remains to be done and further research will no doubt reveal much more than we know at present about this brave people, a large portion of whose history has only survived in their verse.

NOTES

1. Herodotus, IV, 10–42
2. For a fuller discussion of the affinities of Tatar see J. C. Dewdney, *The Turkic Peoples of the USSR* in *The Turkic Peoples of the World*, ed. M. Bainbridge, Kegan Paul, London and New York, 1993, pp. 215 ff.
3. Quoted in A. Khalikov, *Berenche Devlet* (The First State), Kazan, 1991, p. 48
4. See, for example, Yevgeny Kazakov *Об этнокультурных компонентах народов Восточной Европы и Волжской Булгарии*, (On the ethno-cultural components of the peoples of Eastern Europe and Volga Bulgaria) in *Tatar Archaeology*, 1, 1997
5. G. Kuntsevich, *История Казанского Царства или Казанский Летописец* (History of the Kazan Kingdom or the Kazan Chronicle), St. Petersburg, 1905, p. 197
6. Alexandre Bennigsen and Chantal Lemercier-Quelquejay, *Islam in the Soviet Union*, Pall Mall Press, London, 1967, p. 5
7. S. Marjani, *Mustafadel Akhbar fi Ahwali Kazan wa Bulghar*, Vol 1, Kazan, 1897, pp. 80–81
8. *Татар Поэзиясе Антологиясе* (Anthology of Tatar Poetry), Kazan, 1992
9. Mikail bine Ja'far was the son of King Almush of Volga-Bulgaria, who is said to have established Islam as the official religion of the region in 922 AD.
10. For Yasavi (Yesevi) see Alessio Bombaci, *Storia della Letteratura Turca*, Nuova Accademia Editrice, Milano, 1956, p. 76 ff.
11. G. Fleischer, *Catalogus codicum manuscriptorum orientalium Bibliothecae Regiae Dresdensis*, Leipzig, 1831, p. 72, n. 419
12. *Татар Едебияте Тарихы*, (History of Tatar Literature), vol 1, Kazan, 1984, pp. 120–1
13. Kol Sulaiman (also known as Hakim 'Ata) was among the most talented disciples of Yasavi. He lived and worked in Bakyrgan, a village of Khwarezm. See also A. Bombaci, op. cit., pp. 112–114
14. A. Khalikov, op. cit., p. 183
15. See also A. Bombaci, op. cit., pp. 112–114
16. Norton Downs, *Basic Documents in Medieval History*, Toronto, 1959, p. 103
17. *Материалы по истории татарского народа* (Materials for the Study of the History of the Tatar Nation), Kazan, 1995, pp. 139–140
18. *Золотая Орда и ее падение* (The Fall of the Golden Horde), Saransk, 1960

19 For a discussion of the word 'Tatar' see also David Morgan, *The Mongols*, Blackwell, Cambridge/Oxford, 1986, pp. 57 ff.
20 David Morgan, op. cit., p. 57 (with references)
21 M. Usmanov, *Эдигей: Татарский народный эпос* (Edighey, the Tatar popular epic), Kazan, 1989
22 A. Karimullin, *Татары: этнос и этноним* (The Tatars, the ethnos and the ethnonym), Kazan, 1985
23 A. Khalikov, *Татарский народ и его предки* (The Tatar People and their Ancestors), Kazan, 1989
24 Muhammedyar, *Tuhfaye Mardan, Nure Sodur*, Kazan, 1966, p. 61
25 A. Bombaci, op. cit., p. 117
26 M. Safargaliev, op. cit., p. 373
27 A. Bombaci, op. cit., p. 114
28 M. Safargaliev, op. cit., p. 422
29 This epitaph inscribed on the grave of a certain Saitek, son of Jehan Shah (d. 1522) is included in the *Anthology of Tatar Poetry*, vol. 1, Kazan, 1922
30 M. Khudyakov, *Очерки по истории Казанского Ханства* (Essays in the History of the Kazan Khanate), Kazan, 1923, re-print 1997, pp 8–9
31 See R. Bukharaev, *Islam in Russia: The Four Seasons*, Curzon Press Limited, London, 1999
32 *History of Tatar Literature*, op. cit., p. 290
33 Ghayaz Iskhaki, *Идель-Урал* (Idel-Ural), Paris, 1933 (reprinted by the Society for Central Asian Studies, Oxford, 1988, p. 23)
34 For further discussion of *hikmet* see A. Bombaci, op. cit., p. 104
35 K. Fuks, *Казанские татары в статистическом и этнографическом отношениях* (The Kazan Tatars in the Statistic and Ethnographic Profiles), Kazan, 1844, reprint 1991
36 A. Karimullin, *Татарская книга пореформенной России* (The Tatar Book of Reformed Russia), Kazan, 1983
37 M. Friedrich, *Gabdulla Tukai* (1886–1913), Bamberg, 1997, p. 319
38 Ravil Bukharaev, translation by Richard McKane

Volga-Bulgaria to the Golden Horde: 12th–14th Centuries

KOL GALI (QUL 'ALĪ) (1183–1236)

Kol Gali (Qul Alī) was born in one of the cities of Volga-Bulgaria, according to the most recent research, in 1183 AD. He seems to have visited Khwarezm and other parts of Central Asia before returning to his native land at the time of the first Mongol attacks. It is thought that he died in the city of Bilyar in 1236 during the Mongol siege of the city. His only surviving work, the 'Book of Yusuf', a version of the well-known Islamic tale of Yusuf and Zulaikha was completed in 1233. The following extract relates the dream of the Egyptian merchant, Malik, son of Dagir. Yusuf, the Biblical Joseph, has been abducted by his brothers, and in the land of 'Ad has been hidden in a well by Gabriel. Malik dreams of the well and, discovering Yusuf, purchases him as his slave.

The dream of Malik

In Egypt lived a merchant; Malik was his name,
Son of Dagir – and from that noted line he came.
Once Malik had a dream so strange that he became
Intent upon its strict interpretation now.

He called a fortune-teller: 'In my dream', he said,
'I wandered in the land of Canaan, and was led
Towards the well of 'Ad, and from above my head
The sun came down upon the earth before me now.

'I saw it clearly. Yes, it was the radiant sun;
And from my bosom through my collar felt it run.
At once a shower of precious jewels before me spun,
And all those pearls I gathered in my skirt-hem now.

'So gladly did I take those gems, which lay around
And in my purse were all the jewels that I had found.
Such was my dream, O Master of all wisdom sound!
What means this vision? Tell me its great secret now.

The fortune-teller answered: 'Come and sit by me.
The meaning of this dream I shall unfold to thee.
But first give me my payment – pure gold coins – then see!
The dream interpreted will bring thee fortune now.

'If thou hast seen the dream which now thou hast descried,
And in that dream thou founds't thyself by Canaan's side,
Near to the well of 'Ad thou wilt be gratified.
A noble slave will come across thy path – and now

'For little price that slave into thy hands will come.
From this thou shalt receive rewards without a sum.
Then riches follow. Powerful thou wilt become.
For thee such future bliss do I foresee right now.

'The heights of greatness easily shalt thou achieve.
For only in the One Creator men believe,
Who will from bonds of unbelief thy soul relieve.
In both worlds thou wilt find thy glorious riches now.'

The merchant Malik left at once for far-flung lands,
And in the course of time he came to Canaan's sands.
There by a well he set down his great caravans
And waited for the answer to his vision now.

His servants were dismissed from toil and told to rest.
They all dispersed with joy and round the well they pressed.
Then Malik climbed a hill and stood upon its crest
And for the dream to be fulfilled all waited now.

As Malik wandered, suddenly he heard a cry
Emerging from the earth upon the hill nearby:
'Thou wilt find, now hear! when fifty years pass by
The handsome youth, the slave whom thou desirest now.

'Let fifty years pass by and as the heavens turn,
Once more to this same place must thou on time return.
Thou shalt for little price that young slave surely earn
Then sell him at the highest price demanded now.'

Now Malik took the road back home decreed by fate.
Then after fifty years through which he had to wait
Came to that well arriving not a moment late.
And he was joyful, for the time was ready now.

And from the skies above a band of angels fell
Just like a flock of birds they gathered at the well,
Renowned as friends of Yusuf whom they cherished well.
As Malik came, they scattered to the heavens now.

When Malik saw the flock of birds upon the skies,
That they were angels how could Malik realize?
The seeds of faith were hidden from his mortal eyes.
He took his bow to shoot the winged creatures now.

He drew near to the spot; the birds had taken flight.
Poor Malik was amazed their trace had gone from sight.
And then, behold! the well poured forth a wondrous light.
Confused, he stood there, lost for speech, confounded now.

Then Malik went into his tent, and pondering
The essence of this sight, he now saw everything.
He called two trusted slaves and ordered them to bring
Some water from the well: 'And fetch the water now!'

Two slaves, Bashir and Bushra, sprang up straight away
And to the well repaired which was not far away,
And as they lowered their pail for water, strange to say,
They caught the eye of good and righteous Yusuf now.

As they prepared to lower their pail with right intent
And bring the water to their master in his tent,
Gabriel flew down, by the Creator sent,
With tidings of salvation for good Yusuf now.

'O Yusuf', cried the angel. 'did'st thou not once say.
Seeing thy beauty in the mirror on that day:
"If e'er I were a slave then who would pay
A worthy price to settle on my purchase now?"'

'Ah yes', said Yusuf, 'I agree. That did I say.
My image seemed so dear to me upon that day.
I said indeed: "Were I a slave, then who would pay
A worthy price to settle on my purchase now?"'

Then Gabriel replied: 'Stay, wait a while, my friend,
And take this braid; hold tight to it and then ascend.
Merchants wait for thee nearby, and in the end
Thou wilt see thine own true worth. Come with me now.

Bashir and Bushra raised their pails at speedy pace,
And on the water Yusuf showed his comely face.
Who takes the left hand, who the right hand in this race?
The will of the Creator is determined now.

Then from the well the face of valiant Yusuf shone
As beautiful and comely as the radiant moon.
When he beheld it, Malik lost his wits, and soon
Exclaimed: 'Behold! That youth, he stands before us now.'

Many a time had Malik made a declaration
Before his slaves to whom he gave this proclamation:
The first to see that youth will gain emancipation,
And he will have the fair hand of my daughter now.'

When Yusuf's brothers saw men from a distant land
Assembled with their caravan, they formed a band
And said: 'Our slave escaped. Perhaps he is to hand.
We think he might be in your camp with you just now.'

'Now hand him over', cried Ravil. 'No argument!
If not my cry will be to your own detriment.
My deathly shout is feared by all. I'll not relent!
And from it you will also find destruction now.'

But Malik was a cautious man in every way.
He handed Yusuf to his brothers now without delay.
The brothers talked amongst themselves, and straight away
Said: 'Let us sell him as a slave, and do it now.'

This was agreed, and in their Hebrew tongue they said:
To Yusuf: 'We have put a price upon your head
To sell you, otherwise you will be left for dead.
Far better to be sold off to this merchant now.'

Wise Malik quickly comprehended their design
And he rejoiced as he examined every line.
'They'll offer him to me. I'll buy. He will be mine.'
Poor Yusuf groaned. So bitterly he pleaded now.

'And will you really sell me as a slave today?',
Said Yusuf. 'Can you think of driving me away?
And will I curse you for your sins? Will I betray
Your secret? No. It will be safe with me for now.

'Sold to an infidel. Such is my fate. No! No!
This news would break my father's heart, full well you know.
Misfortune's fire will torture me. Be this not so.
Preserve the honour of Khalil. Remember now.'

They answered him: 'Take care! For were our warnings few?
We told our father that a wolf had eaten you.
We lied to Israel; our declaration was not true.
So Yusuf! Do not ask us the same questions now!'

Yehuda helped them talking Yusuf round again.
He said: 'The Lord Himself has sent this awful bane.
Your brothers cannot stop this evil. All's in vain.
If you are obstinate, you see, they'll kill you now.

'Surely better to be sold than fight the fray.
Save yourself and from your brothers keep away.
That dream to see your father might come true one day.
The Lord on High will bless us all in time.' And now

The brothers said: 'Yes, we shall sell him. Never fear!
Now buy him, merchant, take him far away from here.
You shake your purse so freely. If you think he's dear,
We'll surely find another buyer for him now.

Then Malik asked: 'Is he a slave, this handsome youth?
You seem so keen on this transaction. Why forsooth?
What is his sin? What is his fault? Tell me the truth.
In wit and beauty plainly he outstrips you now.'

'Our father bought him as a slave when he was small',
Replied the brothers. 'As a child we loved him all.'
But he turned wanton in his youth; witness his fall.
He ran away and in a well he's hiding now.'

Malik answered: 'Tell me how he went astray;
What are his sins? What is his blame? Now you must say.
Then in this purchase every doubt is cast away.
You must be absolutely honest with me now.'

They said: 'He is indeed a slave. We all agree.
He has three sins: first he absconds, but he's not free;
Then second, he's a thief; he lies, and that makes three.
Purchase him with these three sins, but take him now!'

'I see', said Malik. Your reply, I think, is true.
In spite of what you say, I'll buy this slave from you.
With all his sins and faults some profit might accrue.
Tell me. How much are you asking for him now?

The conclusion of the poem

The story of Fair Yusuf has herein been told
By using Arab themes and Persian tales of old;
And all will read, attending to these worlds of gold.
We ask a simple prayer from our good reader now.

The tale of Yusuf will be spoken by the wise
And all who listen will shed tears from moistened eyes
And cleansed will be their limbs from all their sins and lies
And may the Merciful with grace accept both now.

And if our learned scholars will narrate this tale,
And of its moral men will once themselves avail,
And if in humble prayer they bow and do not fail,
He will accept their meaning and embrace both now.

The reader and the one who hears – they both will pray.
'This poor one is in need of praying', God will say.
Then with their plea so many sins will pass away,
And everyone will be redeemed and pardoned now.

A diamond is a diamond, not an earthly rock;
In vain will fools who cannot see its beauty mock.
And so this tale they may regard as worthless stock,
Yet wiser men will learn much wisdom from it now.

For of this tale indeed, a fool could not conceive;
Its subtle plot the ignorant could not perceive.
But so much did this poor one from its words receive.
May God Almighty recognise its true worth now.

Kol Gali is They servant's name, Oh Lord Benign;
With four and twenty syllables he made each line.
Forgive Thy slave; upon him shed Thy grace divine.
May he send me his mercy, which I hope for now.

In the year six-hundred and thirty was this work complete;
The thirtieth day of Rajab did my labours greet;
I made this shining vault of verse and poetry sweet.
And I received the grace of the Creator now.

THE POEM OF EDIGHEY (14th CENTURY)

The anonymous Poem of Edighey, which laments the fall of the Golden Horde, was probably composed towards the end of the 14th century. Its hero, Edighey, spurred on by pride and ambition, had brought the forces of Tīmur against his former ruler, Khān Tokhtamish. Tīmur's attack brought about the complete destruction of Bolgar the Great and many of the other cities of the region. Tīmur's onslaught was followed by the attack of the Russians under General Fedor Pyostry, who had served in the Russian army at the decisive Battle of Kulikovo in 1380. This was the battle which marked the end of the 'Tatar Yoke'. In the following extract, Edighey's kinsmen, Budai Bey mourns for the devastation of his once glorious land.

The city of Bolgar appears before him;
He does not recognize its altered shape.
The Gates of Victory, on which the verses,
Of the Quran were written, stands agape.

Those holy words engraved in gold are shattered;
The double minarets lie on the ground;
The walls, which stood so high have been demolished
And only dust and ashes fly around.

It seems that no one ever knew this city,
No man nor woman dwelt within its walls.
All has become a sad, deserted wasteland;
No soul is left to grace its hallowed halls.

Not long before, Bolgar was great and famous
With sixty splendid mosques beneath its skies;
Their domes were white as pearls, and so they glinted,
Their precious stones shed light on dazzled eyes.

Those minarets looked down with iron eyebrows;
But now they lie there lifeless without sight.
Edighey came towards them and he saw them,
Demolished, ravaged by the storms of night.

The mosques, the walls, the minarets had crumbled,
And only stones remained to tell their tale.
A pall of smoke hung o'er this once proud city –
A lifeless relic clouded by its veil.

Edighey looked around him from his saddle,
And there he saw his kinsman, Budai Bey,
Who sat with downcast eyes amid the ruins.
Before its time his hair had turned to grey.

Edighey called his name and asked him sadly:
'Why are you sitting in the dust? Your hair
Is white as wormwood from the steppe. Please tell me.
What fate befell your city once so fair?'

With these words Budai Bey gave him the answer:
'You see my hair; you see how it has turned
From black to grey, the colour of the dry steppe.
My youth departed as my city burned.

Jochi, the son of Chingiz, was a warrior,
But still he could not vanquish fair Bolgar;
And then came Batu, grandson of the Great Khan,
To rob our land for plunder near and far.

He took the city, but would not destroy it;
Our holy shrines were conquered but not smashed.
But now the son of Talkh Zabir has trampled
Upon the Moon Gates. See how they lie dashed.

And this is why my hair has turned to silver,
The colour of the steppe-grass, dry and sere.
How else might Budai Bey have greeted fortune,
When you, intent on waging war, drew near?

When you yourself approached with your cruel master,
The son of Baba Tuklas. Hear my sighs!
You, Edighey, came with him to destroy us!
You, Edighey, the light of my own eyes!

How could you lead the Lame One to the palace
Which stood behind the gates of rich Sarai?
How could you join the murderous hordes of Timur,
And bring destruction to our land and sky?

You would not even spare the town of Atryach,
Where coins were minted in the days of old.
You watched the sword cut through the heart of Bolgar,
Where mints once struck its noble coins of gold.

Tokhtamish came at night and with his army
Pulled down the brickwork, redder than the rose.
The city which gave riches to all nations
Was burned to ashes by its cruel foes.

Then after him our country was invaded
By the red-faced Russian Prince, whose bushy beard
Concealed his mouth. His shape was like a dog-fox
Which in the darkest forests had been reared.

He came to plunder like a highway-robber,
And smashed the holy city of Bolgar.
He took Kazan and scaled its lofty portals,
Then breached the vassal-city of Suvar.

Then Juketau, which decorates the River,
And Saby, ringed by forests, were his prey;
He scorched the fields and granaries of Ashly;
Its finest leather goods he bore away.

And coins of gold he raked up with his shovels;
He ravaged houses, then he burned them down.
My land was laid to waste by that cruel tyrant
When he led on his host from town to town.

All fourteen cities of this land demolished!
Reduced to smoke and ashes in a day!
When Budai Bey has witnessed such destruction,
How could his hair from grief not turn to grey?'

HISAM KYATIB (14th CENTURY)

Hisam Kyatib (Hisām Kātib) lived in the second half of the 14th century. He is only known as the author of his poem, Jamjamā Sultān, *'The Skull King'. The story may have been taken from the version of the Persian poet, 'Attār, but the actual source of the poem remains unknown. The Tatar style betrays the poet's intimate acquaintance with Persian.*

The Skull King

Immortals they were called, and so men thought;
But this whole universe will end in naught.

Learn from the times and from the course they run,
For immortality belongs to none.

The signs are clear and tell us that one day
All those who tread this earth will pass away.

And those who lived before our time had started
For good or evil stayed and then departed.

The thousand tribes or kings who ruled alone,
Where are they now, those palaces of stone?

And where is Adam, Noah or Khalil?[1]
All gone, however glorious their seal.

Then Kaikobad, the noblest of the kings;
And Jamshed with his cup of seven rings,

Like Daqiyanus, Shiddad, the Cursed One,
Faridun and Namrud the famous – gone!

Isfandiyar and Rustam are no more;
Naushirvan the Just passed on before.

Mahmud of Ghazna, Islam's noblest scion –
Now who will see his visage wrought in iron?

And where is Ibrahim Adham the Great,
Who changed for poverty his royal state?

---

1 There follows a list of pre-Islamic and Islamic names of saints and kings whose exploits are recounted in Firdausi's *Shāhnāma* and elsewhere

Do Chingiz and Hulagu keep their place
With pagan Bohtinasyr black of face?

They ruled the world and over it held sway;
But hear how they concluded their brief day.

Two pieces of coarse calico their shroud;
Their bodies smeared with blood, no longer proud.

They left behind their wealth, their food, their toys,
Their empires and their thrones and worldly joys.

Whoever walks this earth must go one day,
So men must strive their hardest while they stay.

The world's black soil — and this is plain to all —
Is filled with Adam's children, great and small.

Upon this earth with every step you tread,
You knock your feet against some human head.

In every sweet narcissus that unfurls
Its tendrils there you witness maidens' curls.

And when the hyacinth bursts into light,
You see the locks of kings as black as night.

Beneath the earth how many of them lie
In darkness as their days and nights pass by?

Now one may be a Sultan, others slaves,
Masters, landlords, beggars wretched knaves;

Knights and Shaikhs lie hidden in the sod;
All hoped to find their chosen place with God.

The dust of some upon the wind may run;
The bones of some are whitened by the sun.

For rich and poor are levelled by decay;
And was he slave or sultan? Who can say?

The truth of this by my sweet words is shown;
Their taste like honey in a garden blown.

❖❖❖

One day the Prophet, Jesus, on his way
To Syria, the land where night meets day,

Upon the desert found a verdant mead
With water where the birds flocked down to feed.

He gladly sat beside the restful banks,
And making his ablutions gave his thanks.

At once amid the wastes he saw a stone
On which there was a head now turned to bone.

No eyes, no flesh, no body could be seen,
No limbs left of the man that once had been.

The Son of Maryam slowly turned his eyes
Towards the skull and looked in great surprise.

He cried: 'By Allah! I have never known
A head to be like this of solid bone.'

His words like golden letters rang so clear;
He asked: 'Who are you? How did you come here?

'So much did you accomplish in your day,
But now your soul's sweet bird has flown away.'

Towards the skull then Jesus turned his sight,
And questioned it about its sorry plight.

He asked: 'Dried human head, were you a man
Or woman when your life passed through its span?

'Were you a slave or master or were you
A nobleman or sultan? Tell me true.

And were you rich or destitute or poor,
Or were you homeless, miserable and sore?

Generous or greedy with your share?
Or were you ugly, hideous or fair?'

By Allah's will the skull began its tale;
No teeth or tongue its story to regale.

❖❖❖

'I was a king and ruled in great estate;
I had vast riches and right well I ate.

And when I lived The Skull King was my name;
My justice in the universe found fame.

I had much more besides, and in my time
My capital was known in every clime;

Five days it took to walk its length; three days
Its width to cross; its vastness would amaze.

Within its walls the people of my lands
Had never suffered violence from my hands.

Another palace there I built, so high,
Ten thousand spans it leapt up to the sky.

All praised its beauty looking from outside,
And entering "Like Paradise!" they cried.

And those who climbed its lofty turrets found
Their heads above the clouds that swirled around.

Viziers of forty thousand, noble scions.
Each one of them could fight with royal lions.

Then eighteen thousand Begs, who twice a day
Would join in worship and for fortune pray.

Ten thousand hunting-hawks were in my care;
Strong slaves would tend my dogs and horses there.

Ten thousand cooks belonged to my estate;
I prayed to Allah every time I ate.

To bear my cups ten thousand I would use,
And had ten thousand slaves to make my shoes.

Ten thousand wives I had of royal birth
Each like the sun and moon upon the earth.

Each wife possessed a thousand maids; I paid
A handsome sum for each and every maid.

Each wife was like a houri, fair of face,
And constantly demanded my embrace.

Musicians, seven thousand, played their part,
Each having instruments to show their art.

The dishes at my banquets were supreme.
I miss those feasts as if they were a dream.

My army was a hundred thousand strong;
No mighty force withstood its soldiers long.

My wealth was such that it could not be counted,
And of my banquets stories were recounted.

In those fine days when I was young and fair,
My strength was like a lion's in its lair.

Of diamonds, rubies, pearls there was no dearth.
My name was Skull King – thus my fame on earth.

And all who looked upon my handsome face,
Within their veins their blood began to race.

My countenance – the moon upon the skies –
And in my country I was counted wise.

In others I saw generosity
As inner beauty's outward quality.

I also kept a custom in my time
For which men called me pious and sublime.

If any captive stepped into my court,
If any poor man came, low and distraught,

If dervishes or orphans crossed my moat,
They would receive a horse, a fine fur coat

And many other gifts to soothe their heart
Before the time came for them to depart.

My acts were just and fair; throughout my lands
The whole world was sustained by my own hands.

So many people joined my merry feasts;
Each day for them were killed a thousand beasts,

Then camels in their thousands, horses, sheep;
Both fish and fowl were piled up in a heap.

My cups with wine brimmed over; they were set
With pearls and gems, the finest ever met.

And thus I lived my life in noble state,
But knew that Death would deal me check and mate.'

The dry skull, which had been a king of late,
Thus told the Prophet Jesus of its fate.

Then Jesus put a question to the head:
'My poor narrator, you who are now dead,

When you gave up your soul, what did you see
In Heaven? Please relate your tale to me.

What questions were you asked? Did you receive
Interrogation, comfort or reprieve?

What were the sights of Paradise and Hell?
All that you saw as you passed by, please tell.

And what was your sad end? Can you relate.
If not, then leave these worldly words to fate.'

❖❖❖

'With pomp upon my throne I took my seat;
Each day with me my ministers would meet.

Around me wives and concubines would reign;
One held my crown, another took my train.

You are a man too; mark my words with care.
My glance fell on a pretty damsel there.

I asked her to draw near and stroked her head,
Commanding her at once to share my bed.

Just then a herald came: "Your Majesty!",
He said, "A poor man craves a boon from thee."

But I was angry that he spoilt my pleasure.
For why should worldly matters ruin my leisure?

"You fool! For gifts I have no time", I cried.
"For you nor anybody else beside".

Then to the baths I went to wash away
The grime and the pollution of the day.

As I enjoyed the water's cleansing flow,
Inside my head I felt some illness grow.

Then I collapsed, my sight began to fail;
My very blood ran cold, my face grew pale.'

❖❖❖

'In such a state of misery I lay;
My wealth, my lands and joys seemed far away.

And suddenly I saw my world had changed
Into wilderness where deserts ranged.

Someone appeared; six faces did he show;
His eyes with blood about to overflow.

Both back and forth those faces cast their sight,
Directing it at once to left and right.

His wings to east and west made their appeal;
His name by God decreed was ʿAzrail.

In one hand was a cup, in one a spear;
These symbols were a sign, which made it clear

That he who saw them never would be free
To live in peace and find prosperity.

And with his mortal spear he pierced my breast;
The poisoned chalice to my lips he pressed.

He said: "Your senses you will soon regain,
But tribe and friends you will not see again."'

❖❖❖

The Skull proceeded: 'Jesus, you are wise.
When finally the light came to my eyes,

I saw my body in two cloths was bound;
My flesh was mixed with dust below the ground.

I cried: "Where is my throne? Where is my helm?
My robes and horses, riches and my realm?

My slaves, my concubines! Where have they gone?
The food and drink I used to dote upon?

Without my presence can they be employed?
For only by me were these things enjoyed."

And then the heavenly wall was bathed in light;
Two wondrous angels came into my sight.

In dread I asked: "Who are you? Tell your name."
"We are the Scribes of Heaven", their answer came.

Then from my shroud a scrap they tore away,
And wrote how I had acted in my day.

About my neck they hung it, then they cried:
"Pay for the wrongs you did before you died."

Then devils from the depths of Hell were raised;
About my neck a fiery collar blazed.

They took me by that collar, daubed my face,
And with them to the abyss made me race.

They bound and tied me with a flaming chain,
And cast me to the fire of endless pain.

I suffered as the heat upon me burst;
I cried out for a draught to quench my thirst.

They opened up my mouth and made me drink
A cup of poison filled right to the brink.

I drank it and my liver was on fire;
My inner organs roasted on its pyre.

Once more in me a burning thirst arose;
My blazing flesh began to decompose.

Once more they made me drink that bitter draught.
"No more", I cried. "My mind has gone". They laughed

And pulled me from that fiery place, enchained.
Their cruel blows upon my body rained.

Then from my gaping mouth they tore my tongue,
And stretched it round my neck. And there it hung.

Tormented by their blows, at last I fell.
They dragged me to the very depths of Hell.

◆◆◆

Five hundred men I saw in that grim place;
Their souls were rotting too, and from their face

I realised in panic and alarm
That in their lifetime they had caused much harm.

Beneath them there were other men who lay
Head downwards. Who they were I could not say.

I learnt that they had lived a selfish lie.
And thought of only "I" and "I" and "I".

To learn a thousand trades is given to most;
If you excel in one, why should you boast?

And then I saw a group resembling swine,
Their bellies full of dirt. I could assign

Them to the class of people ever bent
On entering others' lands to sow dissent.

Another group I saw, and they were blind;
They wandered aimlessly without a mind.

Oblivious of themselves, they looked within
And only dwelt upon their guilt and sin.

And tongueless ones there were who could not speak,
And limbless ones who lay there cold and weak.

And those without a tongue had been great kings,
Who ruled unjustly, craving worldly things.

The limbless ones were those who gained high station
By taking up the cause of violation.

More miserable than them another group
Which wandered like a foul, dejected troupe.

Their tongues were hanging out; the pus and blood
Ran from their mouths in one continual flood.

They had dishonoured promises and ties,
And bent the truth with curved and slanting lies.

Another group I saw of tortured men
(I did not count myself among them then).

Their executioners deformed their face
With newly minted coins pressed into place.

The hot gold coins upon their eyes gave pain;
Of face and features nothing could remain.

These were the men who in the world possessed
Great riches, gold and silver, peace and rest,

But for their wealth they never praised God's name.
They had no conscience and they knew no shame.

They never shared the bounty of their days.
See what befell them for their selfish ways.

A man may have a thousand trades, but still
If he is greedy, all will serve him ill.

But if he should be kind, without a trade
For his good deeds he will be well repaid.

Another group roamed in this hellish maze,
Battered by the fire and brimstone's blaze.

These were the shameless bankers we deplore
Who in their life took interest from the poor.

Another group there was — now mark my word —
Which suffered constant torment from the sword.

Their heads were severed from their necks. The Might
Of Allah brought them to this sorry plight.

These were the ones who when they were alive
Shed endless blood and by the sword did thrive.

And others there I saw. Can I recall
Their dismal state? And this the worst of all —

While everyone was clad, these walked about
Quite naked, on their heads nor cloth nor clout.

And blood streamed down their bodies crimson red;
The denizens of Hell looked on in dread.

Full seventy diseases they endured;
Their pus filled ulcers poured and dripped uncured.

And each of them were naked. Who were they?
Now pay attention to the words I say.

From all the seven climes they had come there,
From every country, prosperous and fair,

But never one short garment had they given
To clothe the destitute by anguish driven.

No slave had they released; no charity
Towards those wretched men who would be free.

They would not give a shroud to clothe the dead;
And so they burnt in Hell with naked head.

Remember always when in Hell you burn
Your punishment is what in life you earn.

When Jesus heard this tale of Hell, he wept
And filled with pity there his counsel kept.

❖❖❖

The skull went on: 'My torture never ceased.
I bled and suffered never once released.

Then suddenly I heard a firm decree:
"His term is over. Now he can go free.

Take him from the pit where he has lain
And let his soul find solace from his pain.

Behold his ignorance and feeble mind,
But to his people he was always kind.

To orphans he was merciful and fair;
Both destitute and rich received his care."

They raised me up, and taking Allah's name,
Returned me to the world from which I came.

A thousand years I lived on earth so well;
Four thousand more I suffered down in Hell.

For seventy years worm-eaten I have lain
In this dry valley, treated with disdain.

❖❖❖

Then Jesus said: 'O Head, now tell me true.
Has any other prophet come to you?

The Head replied: 'The Prophet Ilyas
Was our true prophet, but his words, alas!,

We never heeded, nor his God; our own
Mistaken notions we believed alone.

And that is why we drowned in our own blood.
Receiving torment in that fiery flood.'

❖❖❖

Then Jesus answered: 'Make me one request,
And it shall be fulfilled at my behest.'

The Head replied: 'Yes, this is all I ask
To have my body and in health to bask.

In pious worship I desire to live,
So Allah may have mercy and forgive.'

Then Jesus raised his hands up to the skies:
'O Merciful, All-Hearing and All-Wise!

I ask this of Thee: May this one in pain
Retrieve his soul and come to life again.'

Then Allah, Lord of Boundless Might and Wealth,
Gave back the king his body and his health.

❖❖❖

In short, O Son of Adam, from this tale
Learn wisdom and this gift will never fail.

The acts of kings and nobles of the past
Provide you with instruction, which will last.

A man without a purpose lives in vain;
His fame will pass but God's name will remain.

The story of the Skull King has been told.
He reigned in Egypt in the days of old,

A mighty Sultan who achieved great fame,
But to the world he lost his soul and name.

In the seventieth and seven hundredth year
After the Prophet's flight, for people here

Hisam known too as Kyatib wrote this verse
In words instructive and in couplets terse.

ANONYMOUS (14th CENTURY)

The author of the Kisek-bash, 'The Severed Head', one of the most popular poems of 'classical' Tatar literature, is unknown, although, in some later copies, it is often ascribed to one Gali. Its style and diction resemble those of Hisam Kyatib and Kol Gali and may be confidently ascribed to the 14th century. The poem was an essential part of the Tatar school curriculum until 1917. The 19th century Tatar poet, G. Tukai, was inspired to write an amusing parody of the revered poem!

The Severed Head

With *Bismillah*, in Allah's name, we start[1],
Forever keeping God within our heart.

Imagine we are in the time and place
Where Mustafa, our Prophet, lived in grace[2].

This tale in all its beauty let us tell
To warm the hearts of friends and please them well.

The world has seen great wonders in its day,
But nought compared with what we have to say.

This story came upon my tongue so pure.
May Allah help my powers to endure.

One day the Prophet sat with his four friends,
Rejoicing in the blessings Allah sends.

His dear disciples kept his company
(In thousands they were numbered thirty-three).

Then suddenly they saw a severed head,
Which came from nowhere like the tears it shed.

No flesh, but just a head in human guise;
Perhaps a martyr. Tears flowed from its eyes.

Its face was radiant and white its beard.
It fixed them with its dreadful gaze and stared.

---

[1] Bismillah: Arabic: *bismillāhir-rahmānir-rahīm* – 'In the name of Allah the Compassionate and the Merciful' – the first words of the Quran. The formula is pronounced at the commencement of any endeavour

[2] Mustafa: Arabic: Mustafā – 'the Chosen One', a title of the Holy Prophet Muhammad

Beneath the dust its face it would fain hide,
And begged the Prophet's mercy as it cried.

The Prophet was transfixed, but God's Own Lion[3],
The Fearless Ali, entered. Noble scion!

And from the ground he tried to lift the face,
To bring it where the Prophet sat in grace.

No matter how he struggled, he soon found
He could not lift the head up from the ground.

Brave Ali tried; his efforts were in vain.
The Head bewailed and started to complain:

'O Holy Prophet! I appeal to you.
What does this 'Lion of God' think he can do?

He says his strength can equal any test.
Tell him the truth, and let him give me rest.

A thousand men like Ali could be sought,
And act as one, but all would come to nought.

They could not even lift me from the ground,
Or shift me from the earth, which lies around.

For I, when Fate decreed its ordinance,
Was loyal, and saw Allah's countenance.

I know that Allah keeps me in His sight,
And I converse with Him both day and night.

Full fifty times the *Hajj* I have performed;[4]
With alms I helped the hungry and deformed;

The earth I have encompassed on my steed;
To Heaven I have been, and there indeed

I moved amongst the angels; then once more
I took my human likeness as before.

My city was 'The Realm of Light'; my friend
Was Ilyas, who loved me to the end.

---

3 God's Own Lion: The title of the 'Lion of God' (Arabic *Asadullāh*) was given to the Prophet's kinsman, Alī
4 Hajj: the pilgrimage to Mecca, incumbent upon all able Muslims at least once in their lifetime

I had a wife and son of beauty rare,
Who shared my life — such bliss beyond compare!

Alas! A demon ate my son, my soul.
With him he swallowed up my body whole.

He took my wife off to a well so deep
That in my grief I can no longer sleep.

If you will not have mercy upon me,
Henceforth to you no comfort I shall be.'

Quoth Ali: 'This bad deed the *Dev*[5] will rue.
With *Zulfiqar* I'll cut his head in two![6]

And if I fail, this world I shall forsake
And cease to offer prayers that mortals make.'

The Prophet cried: 'Dear Ali, this endeavour
Is bound to fail. You will be lost for ever'.

But Ali answered: 'I must go indeed
And risk my life as Destiny decreed.'

He took his sword and mounted, lion-hearted;
Husain and Hasan wept as he departed.

And all the Prophet's followers that day
Went out with him to see him on his way.

Along with Ali went the Severed Head;
His friends came back; with tears their eyes were red.

On *Duldul* Ali rode. Just see him ride![7]
The disembodied head stayed by his side.

The horse had wings; the people were amazed.
The qualities of Duldul all men praised.

The ritual prayers were said five times a day;
When Ali stopped the Head began to pray.

Together seven days and nights they raced;
At last they reached a drear, deserted waste.

---

5 Dev: in reality a Hindu god, but for Muslims a 'demon'.
6 Zulfiqar: (Arabic *zūlfiqār* – 'the glorious one'), the name of the sword given to Alī by the Prophet
7 Duldul: the name of the mule, on which the Prophet, Muhammad, rode to Heaven

'They saw a well, and Ali asked the Head:
'Is this the well? Is this the place you said?'

'Indeed this is the place; this is the well
In which the evil *Dev* has come to dwell.'

Then Ali glanced at Duldul, full of hope,
For to its saddle was attached a rope.

The rope was lowered, but amid their fears
The Horse and Severed Head burst into tears.

The rope was lowered deeper. Still it ran.
The Severed Head intoned the whole Quran.

One end in Ali's hand, so firm he grips;
The secret name of God is on his lips.

The well is deep; an abyss without end;
He grasps the rope, beginning to descend.

For seven days and nights in that dark well,
He went down to the very depths of Hell.

Eight days went by; his feet touched on the ground.
Bewildered and distraught, he looked around.

Then calling out to God, he fell prostrate;
He looked and there he saw an iron gate.

The gate led to a palace; in that place
He saw a woman with a moon-like face.

And she was praying, hoping that her sigh
Would pierce the darkness and attain the sky.

She bowed in prayer, and doleful tears she shed;
This was the woman of the Severed Head.

And in that palace nought but anguish reigned;
Five hundred Muslims lay there, bound and chained.

They cried to Ali; 'You have come to save
Your wretched people from this evil *Dev*.'

'Who told you of my coming?' Ali cried.
'The Prophet, Mustafa', they all replied.

'He said that you would come to heed our cry,
And at your hands the wicked *Dev* would die.

We were a thousand; now just half remain.
For each day five of us in turn are slain.'

It was not long before brave Ali met
The *Dev*, as lofty as a minaret.

His fingers fat as humans of full girth;
And he had lived a thousand years on earth.

His head was like a dome and badly formed;
Not one good deed in life had he performed.

And from his mouth there came a smoking pall;
One touch of his could raise a city wall.

The demon slept, while Ali raised his sword
To kill his foe without a single word.

'But no!', he said, 'For are you not a Lion?
This deed does not become a noble scion.

It is not right to kill a sleeping foe.
The act is evil. This you surely know.'

He shouted once. The *Dev* still slumbered deep;
The manly cry could not disturb his sleep.

The Warrior of Allah called once more;
The mountains trembled at that awful roar.

The *Dev* awoke at last and looked around,
And from his flaming mouth there came a sound:

'So you have come to sow the seeds of strife.
At Ali's hands will I now loose my life?

No! I shall strike you first, and never fear.
But tell me, Ali, who has sent you here?'

Then Ali answered: 'It was Allah's will
That I should come; I am empowered to kill.'

The Dev replied: 'No! It is I who slay.
No Muslim will survive when I hold sway.

The Prophet too shall perish at my hand;
Medina, even Mecca will not stand.'

He spoke as fate decreed, and raised his mace,
Which weighed a thousand tons. Then face to face

With Ali he joined battle on that field,
Protecting his own body with his shield.

The mace descended with a frightful sound,
And Ali sank waist-deep into the ground;

But never once was Ali's hand deflected,
Nor for a moment was his heart dejected.

He freed himself, and on a rock he stood,
Still praising Allah, who is Great and Good.

The Dev cried out: 'So, Ali, will you slay
One such as I? And is this why you pray?

You might be like the Caucasus, my friend,
But I shall cut your body end to end!'

Three times he struck, but Ali did not fall.
So strange! His blows had no effect at all.

And now came Ali's turn to make a stand;
His sword, great Zulfiqar, was in his hand.

He cried: 'Just lift one finger up to me,
And then the Truth of Allah you will see.'

The Dev replied: 'I've lived a thousand years,
But never once with worship and such fears

Have I been troubled. Never in my days
Have I known faith, obedience or praise!

I'll never bow to Allah. If I die,
This question of belief will pass me by.'

And when he heard the demon scoff and mock,
Brave Ali, angered, stepped down from his rock.

He chopped his head off with a single blow,
And thus condemned the spirit of his foe.

The Lion of God thus slew the mighty Dev,
Whose soul from black perdition none could save.

At this, the palace doors burst open wide,
And other *devs* rushed Ali from each side.

But Ali was prepared to face them all,
Determined now that all of them would fall.

Their heads began to roll in every place,
And Ali trampled on each ugly face.

Three hundred *devs* were slaughtered in that fray.
The Lion of God, the Hero of the Day!

The other demons saw this awful sight;
To save their lives they ran away in fright.

They could not bear to face this Man of Stone;
They fled and Ali found himself alone.

And then five-hundred Muslims came. They took
The spoils and treasure which the *devs* forsook.

As much as they could carry, this they brought,
And then a road up from the well they sought.

They cried: 'Dear Ali, this well is so deep.
How can we climb its walls so sheer and steep?

For we possess no wings to help us fly;
No ladder do we have to reach the sky.

It seems that we are doomed to perish here.
What else does fortune hold for us but fear?'

The Ali said: 'Now pray that you may live.
Deliverance is only God's to give.'

And he himself fell down in humble prayer;
His supplication flew up to the air,

Traversing all nine heavens. Gabriel
Was told to spread his wings and speed them well.

When Ali's prayer was finished, they all found
Themselves on earth, their feet upon the ground.

Five-hundred Muslims, men and women, sang
Their praise of Ali; from their hearts it rang.

Then Joy and Happiness replaced their fear.
And all of us can find a lesson here.

And when this news the Holy Prophet learned,
That Ali, God's Own Lion, had returned,

They all went out to meet their noble friend;
Their praise of the Almighty knew no end.

The Severed Head approached; the Prophet took
Him in his hands, and with a kindly look

Asked mercy for him from the Lord above.
The prayer found favour in eternal love.

The Severed Head became a man once more,
With hands and legs and body as before.

To see him whole the company was dazed;
By Allah's miracle all were amazed.

His poor son's flesh the demon had consumed;
Now only bones were left to be entombed.

But God bestowed on him a body too,
And decked him out in raiment fresh and new.

Maulana Shams Tarazi is our Light[8];
And in his memory do what is right.

This rhythmic verse was written for his sake.
Now seek Salvation and this world forsake.

---

8 Shams Tarazi: spiritual guide of the great poet Maulānā Rūmī, presumably also the author's spiritual guide

SAIF-I SARAI (c.1321–1396)

Saif-i Sarai was born in the small Volga town of Kamyshly, and later moved to Sarai where he began his poetic career. Perhaps in order to escape the plague, he migrated to Egypt and became a scribe at the Mamluk court. There he wrote his major works: a version of Sa'dī's Gulistān *and the romance of* Suhail and Geldersen. *A number of ghazals and qasīdas are also found in his manuscripts. Like that of his contemporaries, his verse exhibits the influence of Persian writers.*

The Dawn Qasīda[1]

The eagle of the dawn spread out its golden wings;
The stars like timid doves were chased across the sky;
The morning like the hosts of great Byzantium
Dispelled the darkness crushing all its ranks on high.

The scalpel of the dawn cut through the heart of night
And filled the vault of Heaven with its scarlet blood.
The birds took wing; the whole world joined in praise
And called 'Allahu Akbar' – 'See how great is God'[2].

The earth became as beautiful as Paradise;
The vast celestial dome spun like a lover crazed.
The flowers were moist with dew, and as they drank
In wild intoxication their Creator praised.

The dew upon the rose glowed red like ruby wine
And opened up the petals to the nightingale,
Which sang lamenting to the tender strings of dawn;
Rare scent was spread abroad by the narcissus pale.

The cypress stood as tall as the beloved fair[3]
And gently waved its boughs like arms in reverie;
The fragrant morning breeze towards the garden flew;
The whole world's brain was drunk in perfumed ecstasy.

---

1 qasīda: an ode of varying length usually written in praise of one's patron, a saint, God and the Prophet, or some other dignitary. The qasīda is one of the most popular verse forms in Arabic and Persian.
2 Allāhu Akbar: Arabic 'God is the Greatest', a phrase commonly used in the call to Prayer and during supplications
3 cypress: the stature of the beloved is often compared to the tall, elegant cypress

And I was in the midst of all that broke around.
When suddenly that Beauty known to those in love
Strayed upon the scene; the cypress kissed her feet;
Her waving locks gave fragrance to the air above.

The wonder of the day inspired this ode of mine;
My verse recalled the glory of those times now passed –
The Alexandrian Princes, their benevolent ways,
The Seal of Prophets, and of all the Prophets last[4].

It tells the tales of Rustam in the Age of Lions[5];
Such heroes from this earth departed long ago.
The days when valiant Mahdi would display his might.
In our poor age could we such acts of courage know?

The source of all munificence, the fount of joy,
When by yourself proceeding like a knight in chess
Could with one single arrow decimate your foes
And then upon their fleeing armies torment press.

And those you entertained in games of chess and nard[6]
Beheld their world become a garden rich and fine;
And Zuhra at your feast revealed the strains of love[7];
The crescent moon so young regaled your guests with wine.

Saif-i Sarai shall also sing your highest praise[8];
His rhythm has the purity of pearls so white;
He sang this ode of adulation when the dawn
Unsheathed its sword and cut the curling locks of night.

The morning breeze will always chase the fleeting clouds;
The wind of grief will ever blow throughout the land;
But let brave men still speak their fathers' noble tongue
And on their horses vie and triumph hand in hand.

---

4 The Seal of the Prophets: the Holy Prophet Muhammad is believed, by all Muslims, to be the last Law-bearing Prophet of God
5 Rustam: one of the pre-Islamic heroes, whose prowess is described by Firdausī in his *Shāhnāma*, 'the Chronicle of Kings'.
6 Nard: a game
7 Zuhra: the planet Venus, a symbol of dazzling beauty
8 Saif: the Arabic word for 'sword'

Ghazals

Ah! Why has fate made me a slave to its dark spell?
My name is Saif — a sword held in the scabbard's cell.

She sees a virtuous man and will not lift her eyes;
But worthless knaves she courts and praises to the skies.

My words she counts as priceless pearls and holds them dear;
She takes them greedily and hides them in her ear.

A moon-faced beauty cunningly bewitched my soul
And held me with the magic of her dusky mole[1].

No beauty in this world can with her looks compare,
And constantly she lures admirers to her snare.

Her skills are great, her habits are beyond reproach;
She will not let the ones who dote on her approach.

Saif-i Sarai burns in the flames of separation.
Still gazing at that moon in hope of consolation.

❖❖❖

Like curling hyacinths the locks of my beloved flow[2];
Her face — a perfumed garden in which flowers ever grow.

Her stature is a stately cypress standing straight and tall;
Her cheeks are red as roses when in spring the fresh buds blow.

Her golden words enhance the beauty of the early dawn;
Her grace and charm the men who live in far-flung China know.

Ennobled by descent, her words are true, but Turkish eyes[3]
Wreak havoc on her lovers, and like Tatars lay them low.

My soul becomes a portal for the envoys of her love;
They enter and soon find the prison where all lovers go.

My heart scorched by the flames of love is constantly on fire;
And from my eyes without abating tears of amber flow.

❖❖❖

---

1 mole: in Persian verse on the cheek is regarded as a sign of beauty
2 hyacinth: the curling locks of the beloved are compared to the hyacinth (*sunbul*)
3 Turkish eyes: in Persian poetry, the Turks, and the Tatars in particular, have beautiful eyes, but are equally noted for their treachery and cruelty

Her face is like the moon, the soul of all we see;
The queen of all known beauty in this age is she.

And bathed in jasmine she stands like a cypress fair;
Her locks to heaven's perfume hold the sacred key.

Her golden lashes turn her lovers into slaves,
And like the circling moon her eyes make sorcery.

The arrows of her glances pierce the wounded heart;
The whole wide world falls victim to her archery.

Each day the sun arises from her collar torn,
And that is why the earth grows bright with luxury[4].

So let the hoar-frost freeze the soul of him who loves;
Her moon-like grace condemns all souls to slavery.

Saif-i Sarai! You are her slave; behold her charms.
The wonder of the works of God Most High is she.

---

4   collar torn: the torn collar is a sign of the lover's distraction and anxiety; it is often compared to the ragged white line of the false dawn

The Kazan Khanate: 15th–17th Centuries

MUHAMMAD AMIN (AMĪN) (1460–1518)

Muhammad Amin, who is regarded as one of the most enlightened rulers of Kazan, ascended the throne of the Khanate in 1487 with the assistance of the Grand Prince of Moscow, Ivan III, who is said to have treated him like an adopted son. His long reign brought an end to the civil disorder and bloody feuds which had continued for 21 years prior to his accession.

The calamity

In the year seven hundred and fifty after the Hijra
An earthquake great and mighty shook the world;
This lame and craven man with the mind of an idiot
Brought suffering and despair to every house.
How many shaikhs and scholars fell as martyrs
Beneath the sweet effulgence of Islam!
The world was ruined; Islam lay broken, shattered,
And tears like rivers flowed down every cheek.
Now what will be his answer before Allah
When he is questioned for his evil deeds?
O God! Wouldst Thou reward that slave of Thine
With pains and torture in the life to come!

ÖMMI KAMAL (SECOND HALF OF THE 15th CENTURY)

Ömmi Kamal is mentioned in the Ottoman archives and it is thought that he may have been a wandering dervish of the Shaikh Bahavetdin school. We know that he died in 1475. His poems are composed in Seljuk Turkish, but are said to contain elements of Tatar-Kipchak. He talks of the former territories of the Golden Horde, including Kazan and the Crimea as 'alien lands', but the small portion of his verse which has come down to us has always fascinated and indeed influenced Kazan Tatar poets even down to the 20th century. Ömmi Kamal's rich descriptions of nature and its beauty are among the first of their kind to be attested from the time of the Kazan Khanate:

Spring

From Paradise a gentle breeze began to blow;
The dead lands came to life, and those who slept revived;
And every field and meadow took upon itself
Its former glory which the Artist had contrived.

And all around was beautified with wondrous hues,
White, yellow, black, vermilion, red and green;
The Guardian of Paradise unlocked his gates;
All was transformed, and Heaven upon this earth was seen.

And every creature praises Allah in its way;
Beasts roam the valleys; birds regale the air with song.
Amid the flowers the nightingale sang of his love;
Upon the rose he perched; his lay was sad and long.

So hard he strove his praise and wonderment to show,
In ecstasy he fell down to the grass below.

PLATE 2 A Kazan Tatar, 15th – 17th centuries

PLATE 1 A Bulgar, 8th – 9th centuries

PLATE 3 A Kazan townswoman, mid-16th century

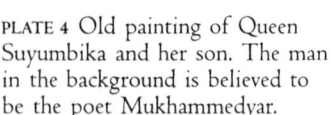
PLATE 4 Old painting of Queen Suyumbika and her son. The man in the background is believed to be the poet Mukhammedyar.

PLATE 5 A Kazan Tatar, 18th century

PLATE 6 A Kazan Tatar, 19th century

PLATE 7 Art Nouveau style costume of a Kazan Tatar, beginning of the 20th century

PLATE 8 Samples of fine calligraphy, a Persian Divan, 1800s

PLATE 9 Frontispiece of a mid-19th century manuscript by calligrapher Ali Makhmudov

PLATE 10 Ornamental headpiece in watercolour for a 19th century Qur'an

PLATE 11 Manuscript page by calligrapher Ali Makhmudov and an advertisement prospectus by V. Varaksin (right), mid-19th century

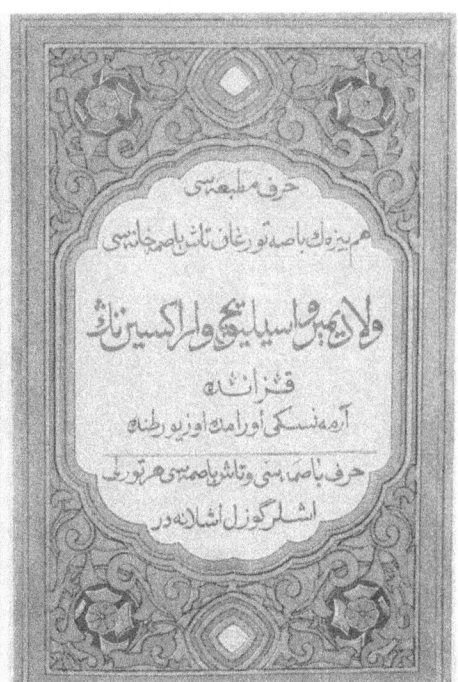

PLATE 12 Samples of shamail wall panels by calligrapher G. Saliev, beginning of the 20th century

PLATE 13 The Smaller Minaret of Bolgar the Great, 14th century

PLATE 14 The Black Chamber, believed to be a school or some other public institution of Bolgar the Great, 14th century

PLATE 15 The Khan's Tomb or the Eastern Mausoleum of Bolgar the Great, 14th century

PLATE 16 'Kazan of Old', oil painting by Ravil Zagidullin

PLATE 18 The minaret of the Azimov Mosque in Kazan

PLATE 17 The Azimov Mosque in Kazan, built 1887-90

PLATE 19 The Hay Market Mosque of Kazan, built in 1849

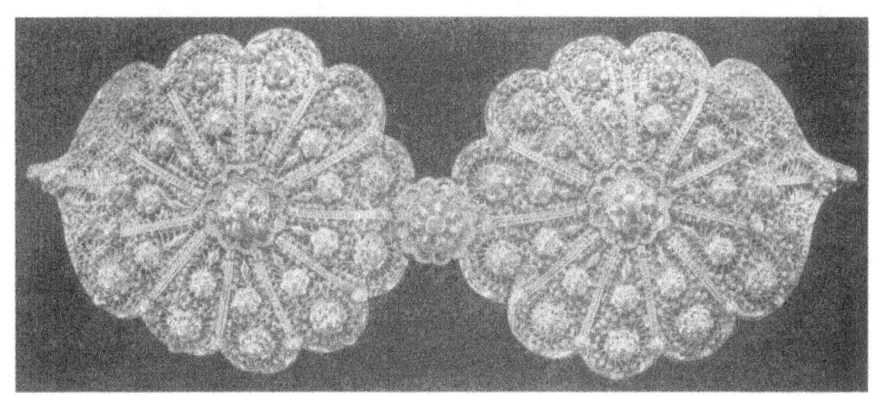

PLATE 20 Kazan Tatar belt-buckle in gold filigree

PLATE 21 Section of foliate belt-buckle, set with jewels

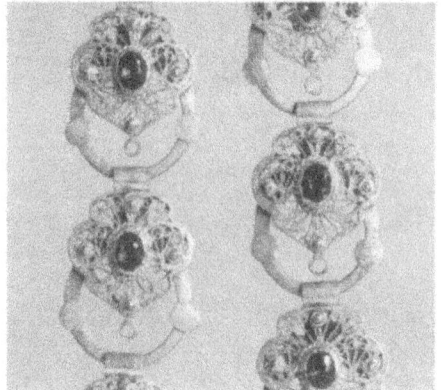

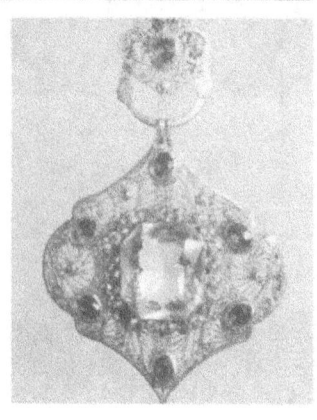

PLATE 22 Silvergilt collar pendent in open-work filigree

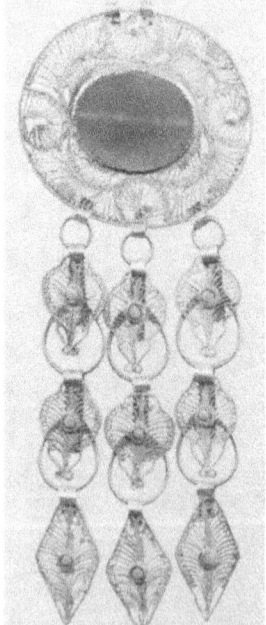

PLATE 23 Ajoure silvergilt brooch with triple foliate pendants

PLATE 24 Napkin worked with coloured silks in chain stitch

PLATE 25 Tablecloth corner worked with coloured silks in chain stitch

PLATE 26 *Orpek* national head covering, embroidery in chain stitch

PLATE 27 Velver skullcap with tassel, worked with chain-stitched gold thread, bullion, twisted metal wire and paillettes

KOL SHARIF (d.1552)

Kol Sharif, after his father's death became the leader of the local Muslims in his place. He is said to have perished in the final battle for Kazan when the Muscovite army was met with the resistance of a handful of defenders at the Kol Sharif Mosque. Most of the city's archives and manuscripts were lost in the fire, which followed the Russian attack, but a few of Kol Sharif's poems survived.

Ghazal

My soul! Do not yield to the world.
This world is for ever constrained;
And all those who live in this world
To the goblet of death are chained.

Do not fancy that you will remain
In this world for long; for its fire
Is kindled and blazes anew
With the flames that will burn your pyre.

For none of us knows whence we came,
And whither we go, can we know?
There is no beginning or end,
But the loan must be paid ere we go.

Kol Sharif! Your mother and sire
Were a good deal wiser than you.
For if you make friends with this world,
You will lose the reward, which is due.

MUHAMMEDYAR, ALSO KNOWN AS MAHMŪD KHOJĪ (16th CENTURY)

Muhammadyar or Mahmūd Khojī lived in the Kazan Khanate during the first half of the 16th century. At the court of Kazan he composed his two longest works: Tohfaye Mardan (Tuhfa-i Mardān) 'The Gifts of Young Men' (1539) and Nuri Sodur (Nur-i Sudūr) 'The Light of Breasts'. He may have died during the storming of Kazan by Ivan the Terrible in 1552. In much of his work he takes a strong moralistic stance.

The fate of a girl

There lived a King of boundless power and might,
Whose life was blessed by riches and delight.

Iskandar[1] might have put him to the test.
But still he would have vanquished East and West.

And with his retinue as night came down
The King would walk the dark streets of his town,

Amid the dwellings of his subjects there
To find out who was bad and who was fair.

And in his thirst for knowledge one dark night
He came across a house all bathed in light.

Before his eyes there was a wedding feast;
The throng of women in the yard increased.

And in their midst, with knitted brows, two men
Sat there in readiness – each had a pen.

A wondrous picture, but the strangest thing –
No one beheld this sight save for the King;

Nor feast, nor writers, nor the nuptial cheer.
The King was seized against his will by fear.

Around that magic hall the circle bright
Would now be gone, and now drift into sight.

Then sternly did the King these strangers ask:
'Come tell me, in the name of God, your task.

---

1 Iskandar: Alexander the Great

'We are but writers', they replied, 'and we
Record what is ordained by Heaven's decree.

'Now see our host's young daughter standing there;
She will amaze you with her beauty rare.

'One glance, while half asleep or half awake,
Would seal the fate of any man and make

'His soul her captive. She is soft and calm;
Her comeliness would soothe the heart like balm.

Just like the crescent moon that face so fair;
With such a rose could any bloom compare?

Her lips so delicately carved and framed;
Before them Egypt's daughters are ashamed[2].

But on her fourteenth birthday, at that hour[3],
A wolf will come and that fair maid devour.'

At that they disappeared with no more word.
The king was grieved by all that he had heard.

In tears he waited for the dawn to rise,
All night that strange abode before his eyes.

Forgetting everything but grief and sorrow,
He hurried there once more upon the morrow.

Her father he paid well, and took the maid
Into to his sumptuous palace where she stayed.

No daughter blessed the master of this throne;
He cherished her as if she were his own.

He doted on her, showed her love so rare,
And gave her every luxury and care.

Her beauty had no equal; just one glance
From her struck young men like a deadly lance.

---

2 Egypt's daughters: a reference to the Egyptian slave-girls of Zulaikha who fell in love with Yūsuf (Joseph)
3 fourteenth birthday: in Persian tales, a child's fourteenth year is considered dangerous, since it is the time of puberty, when the child is prone to falling in love. To offset the danger, the child is kept apart from the world, but fate can never be cheated.

Her winning smile, the mole upon her cheek
Drove people mad and made the senses weak.

Not for a moment could our Sovereign bear
To be without his moon-faced darling fair.

Her fourteenth year would bring him desolation;
From cruel fate could there be no salvation?

The king himself knew what had been foretold,
And challenged destiny with measures bold.

From every land to his own realm he brought
The finest architects who could be sought,

And ordered them to build a palace there
Outstripping Paradise, beyond compare.

Then water, food of every kind and taste
Within a golden chest inside he placed

With artful keys he locked the chest away,
And it was lit by candles night and day.

'My daughter', said the King, 'for one whole year
Safe from the cursed wolf will you live here.

After that time, if you are still alive,
And from the hand of fate and death survive,

When that day dawns, you shall be called my own
And you will have my sceptre and my throne.'

Into this mansion passed the fairy-maid,
Then iron and rock before its door were laid.

The King said: 'There can be no harm or wrong;
No wolf could enter through such portals strong.'

In time the King thought of his daughter fair:
'Why should she be alone and suffer there?'

He sought a country maiden, live and free,
To give the princess joyful company.

She went inside, the house was sealed once more;
With lead and stone they fastened up the door.

So happily the two young girls resided,
Enjoying all the luxuries provided.

They entertained each other every day
By telling stories, lost in games and play.

The country-girl grew curious in the end
To know the secret of her royal friend,

And asked the princess in simplicity:
'Why have they robbed you of your liberty?'

'Why this strange place? Unburden your sad heart.
To me this secret will you not impart?'

The princess answered: 'You must know, my friend,
For you have shared my exile to this end,

Once in His wisdom Allah made it plain
That by a savage wolf I will be slain.

When God gives me the life that I am due,
Then I shall see that all your dreams come true.'

The simple girl cried out: 'O Heavenly Lord!
Before Thee I am pure. Now hear my word:

Supposing I became that wolf for Thee?'
The Judge on High attended to her plea.

And when that year ordained by Heaven had passed,
The people thronged to know her fate at last.

The doors were opened of the dungeon's room;
All fled – they saw a she-wolf in the gloom.

The country-girl had turned into a beast;
White bones remained the remnants of her feast.

The King, consumed to ashes by this sight,
Addressed the Sole Possessor of All Might:

Against Thy will, O Lord, no man can win.
Forgive my pride, for I shall no more sin.'

On goodness

Take courage now! Do good! You must make haste.
From goodness you will have the sweetest taste.

When bargaining, then call a spade a spade.
Dishonesty with evil is repaid,

In doing good you have so much to gain.
For vengeance is the evil-doer's bane.

Let him who tires in conflict be your friend.
To you one day he might his hand extend.

'My enemy will not do good', you say.
But know, tomorrow is not yesterday.

A song-bird in a cage if you should see,
Have pity on the wretch and set it free.

All men esteem the goodness that you do,
And pay you back in full with goodness too.

A dialogue between the poet and his heart

One day as I was sitting in my room
And drinking deeply from the cup of gloom,

Burnt in the fire that blazed within my heart,
A trembling prisoner, grieved and torn apart,

I cried: 'My heart, be calm. Do not torment
My soul. Now give me peace. Relent!'

My heart replied: 'Remember, God commanded
That I should rule you. Thus it was demanded.

'Since I am in the centre, my position
Dictates that I should offer admonition.

'Muhammad Yar, your tongue's a nightingale;
The whole world is its garden to regale.

'It's hard to talk in verse. You have no blame.
But harder still to hide the inner flame.

'How many there have been whose speech was dear!
The pearls they sowed with words still flourish here.

'But others ached in silence, grieved alone;
The value of their words remains unknown.'

'Allow me', I replied, 'insistent Heart,
If you will be so kind, to say my part.'

'So many wretched men live in this town,
Unknown to others, miserable, cast down.

'Should I forget the place from which I came,
And impudently seek the halls of fame?

'This is the reason why I am so meek.
And if it is not given me to speak

'With inspiration, passion for repute,
So what? Far better to sit deaf and mute.

'So many have aspired to enthral,
And think that they are poets, great and small.

'Their boasting sickens me. Their time has passed.
Be silent! Let me be myself at last.'

'No, you will be the fool', my heart replied,
If you stay silent, casting me aside.

'Speak out and share your talent, lest you fall,
And let your goodness be a gift to all.

'Devote yourself to love, be kind and fair;
Spread wide your tightened girdle if you dare.

'Let God behold your courage and its sum.
Vainglorious singers you shall overcome.

'Share out your treasured goods in every place,
For only selfish scoundrels hide their face.'

I heard these words, and I was filled with shame.
I said: 'God will forgive me for this blame.

'You know my thoughts and you are always right.
Now let me keep the glorious path in sight.

'Let my sweet words win triumph from above,
And with my verse may people fall in love.'

A husband and wife who spun and sold their yarn

By the grace of the Lord if a tongue
  For true speech I deserve,
I shall tell you a tale, which is meant
  For instruction to serve.

You may leave, Yar Muhammad, the truth
  Of the tale in our care.
To their target the arrows unfailingly
  Speed through the air.

With your poesy brighten my face,
  Poet, schooled in the art.
Of this land, Yar Muhammed, your verse
  Will enrapture the heart.

❖❖❖

Now there once lived a man with his wife;
  They were poor and quite old.
And the town where they lived had the name
  Of Farkhar, so I'm told.

If the Lord God was kind, and they earned
  A few pennies, they ate;
But if nothing they earned, they would have
  To go hungry and wait.

Just how long they continued to live
  In this way, I can't say,
But it happened they got a bit extra
  To play with one day.

For half of the sum the old man bought
  Some millet and bread;
While the wife with the other half bought up
  Some cotton instead.

From the cotton the woman wove yarn,
  Never sparing her strength.
And the man went to market next day
  To dispose of the length.

Now that was their business, and that's
   How they spent all their days.
They were grateful to Allah and never
   Neglected His praise.

It so happened the husband went off
   With his yarn one fine day
To sell it and purchase their food
   In the usual way.

And as he returned with his goods,
   From the road came a shout;
There were two people brawling. The reason
   He went to find out.

Curiosity prompted his question:
   'Now tell me, good sirs,
Just why are you fighting each other,
   Behaving like curs?'

They told him that one earned a shilling;
   The other one said
He had lost it. The first didn't trust him;
   That's why he saw red.

The old man was vexed: 'You are foolish
   And equal in blame.
When over a shilling you perjure
   Your family's name.'

Then he took out a shilling, and handing
   It over went on,
Saying: 'God will reward me for kindness
   When everything's gone.

And when he came home, he looked humble
   And said to his wife:
'Now, my dear, don't be angry, but
   Pity my miserable life.'

Then he mentioned the shilling, and told
   The whole truth in the end.
The woman was moved by his story
   And said: 'My dear friend.

'You have done good indeed, and the Lord
    Will look kindly on you;
It is He who has shown you the path,
    Which is righteous and true.

'We must therefore be grateful to Him
    Who has given us life;
Surely God has rewarded us.' Such were
    The words of his wife.

Overjoyed, the old man heard these words;
    All was sweetness and light.
And his heart filled with gladness to know
    That he'd done something right.

Soon their money ran out; there was no one
    Who wanted to pay.
And so they sat hungry with nothing
    To eat for that day.

Then the woman decided to gather
    The combings she found,
And all through the night she wove yarn
    From the scraps on the ground.

She then turned to her husband and said:
    'That is all I can do.
Go and sell it. At least we shall eat
    If some money comes through.'

In the market he had no such luck;
    The reaction was cold.
And the customers passed by the yarn,
    Which was covered in mould.

Without selling his yarn he went homewards,
    And what did he see?
A downcast Jigit[1] sitting there
    With a fish on his knee.

---

1 Jigit: the Turkic word simply means 'young man'; in poetry, the Jigits are famed for their honour and prowess

'Are you selling your goods?', he enquired,
    Half concealing his wish.
'If you are, take this yarn in exchange
    And I'll purchase your fish.'

The Jigit had been there with his fish
    Since the break of the day.
'Well then, give me your yarn', he replied.
    'Take my poor fish away.'

As so holding the fish, the old man took
    The road to his house;
And before his old wife he sat humble
    And quiet as a mouse.

'See, the yarn wouldn't sell. It was mouldy',
    He dolefully said.
'In the end I exchanged it and purchased
    This fine fish instead.'

'Never mind', said the woman. 'The fish
    Will provide us our fare.
'We'll give praise to the Lord and contritely
    We'll thank Him in prayer.'

Then they found a clean place for the fish,
    And adroitly the wife
In the name of the Lord cut its belly
    Apart with her knife.

The old woman cried out to her husband:
    'Just look what I've found!
There are pearls in the fish. See what quality,
    Sparkling and round!

She now gazed at her treasure and placed
    The fine gems in a bowl:
'Take these pearls to the jeweller in secret,
    And don't tell a soul!'

The jeweller marvelled and asked the old man
    Whence they came.
But he humbly replied he'd received them
    By taking God's name.

Then the jeweller said: 'You must take them
 To no other shelf.
I am ready to buy them for three hundred
 Thousand myself.

'I'll add five hundred more. I can see that
 These pearls are not trash.
But give them to me and I promise
 I'll pay you in cash.

The old man gave his pearls to the jeweller
 And left with the money.
As he made his way homewards, his mood
 Was decidedly sunny.

He stamped over the threshold, and what
 A commotion he raised!,
Calling out to his wife in a shout: 'Look!
 We're rich. God be praised!'

❖❖❖

And now they were free from the
 Bitterest travails of life;
From the hunger that pressed them; the needs
 Of the world and its strife.

And in peace they would talk of the
 Happiness, which was now theirs;
'For the rest of our lives we shall live
 Far from poverty's snares.'

At that moment there thundered a voice:
 'Hear this homeless one's plea!
Turn your ears to this wanderer. Will you
 Have pity on me?'

'I am wasted by hunger, and barefoot
 And naked I go;
I have none to protect me, and Fate
 Deals me blow after blow.

'Give me water and bread, and a penny
 If you've one to spare;
When you die, you will be well rewarded
 In Paradise fair.'

They both looked at each other, and said:
    'Shall we call him inside?'
'Please Come into our home, wretched man.
    As our guest you'll reside.

'God rewarded us well with great riches
    Against expectation.
Now we'll share half our wealth with you,
    Ending your sad desolation.

'Take your part of this Heavenly bounty,
    And then come what may,
Every joy will be yours, and your face
    Will be brightened today.

On generosity

O diamond, fount of generosity!
Rare diamond hidden in contentment's sea!

Such generous feelings fully to explain
I open up the book to make them plain.

Pay heed to words of generosity;
The source of joy more clearly will you see.

The generous man, content with his own place,
The light of happiness will bathe his face.

Who, freely giving, hopes his soul to save
Will never fall to Hell beyond the grave.

He who from the heights of skill looks down
Wears his achievements like a royal crown.

Wise pillars of the Majlis[1]! Here for you
My homily; for your electors too.

Since generosity redeems all sin,
The good man finds his profit placed therein.

In this world and the next is his reward;
For God will take him as his special ward.

---

1 Majlis: a Muslim assembly

MEVLA (MAULĀ) KOLY (17th CENTURY)

Mevla (Maulā) Koly, also known as Bairam 'Ali Koliev lived during the second half of the 17th century. Born to a family of Cossack Tatars in a village near Kazan, he became head of a newly established Tatar settlement near the ancient city of Bilyar. The settlement was removed on the order of Peter the Great in 1699, after which nothing is known of Maulā Koly. Much of his verse, in keeping with the style of his day, is didactic and moralistic.

On tramps

God save me from leading the life of a tramp;
I would not wish others the trouble they see.
No roof overhead and no comforting lamp;
Their lot is to suffer; no peace can there be.

A tramp is a man for whom no others care;
But we have our home and with guests often share
The pleasure of friendship and company rare.
But a tramp only sees this in dull reverie.

No father to honour, no age to revere;
No mother to burden with worry and fear;
And none to enquire of his health or to cheer.
The death of a tramp is the worst you will see.

He lives all alone, and alone he will die,
With no one to bury him, no one to cry.
The years he has lived to oblivion fly.
Such death is as sad as no other can be.

Love, passion and morality

To her I devoted my soul and my mind;
We meet, she ignores me and knows not my name.
I burn in the fire of a love that is blind;
No water from her to extinguish the flame.

My heart may boil over; she has not a care;
'Mid thousands of others she sees not my fame.
She came and she kindled and made the coal flare;
No passion for passion with her all the same.

I turned into ashes, but failed to inspire;
She will not become either radiance or fire

On kinsmen

If the love of your kinsmen is steadfast and true,
Then existence is sweeter than sugar for you.

Relations share secrets; in them you confide.
If you're challenged in battle, they'll stand by your side.
Supportive in business, they last and abide.
For a man without kinsmen the pleasures are few

This world

Unto this world pay no great heed;
It beckons with its bright allures,
But thwarts your every work and deed.
Here only cruelty endures.

All fades like mist at morningtide,
And like the mask that decks a bride-
So charming! But what does it hide?
This world all honesty obscures.

The truth it bids you to forget;
It leads you from the path you've set
Into its own deceptive net.
This world with cunning ever lures.

One thing awaits us when we leave –
The grave! And there is no reprieve.
We disappear. But will you grieve?
The world in badness e'er endures.

Preface to the *Hikmet*[1]

One thousand and eighty and eight was the year
When the *Hikmet* was written, and 'Wisdom' was named.
In the town of Bolgar on the River's fair banks,
By the great sinner Koly whose life will be blamed.

---

1 Hikmet: The hikmet was a genre of Turkish verse employed in ritual chanting. Mevla Koly's Hikmet, 'Wisdom', was apparently composed ion 1088 Hijri = 1677 AD.

My days were all cheerless and doleful, my friends;
The tears from my eyes dug a path for their way.
I am gnawed by remorse and repent day and night.
My Lord! When the Judgement comes, what shall I say?

All my deeds caused displeasure to Heaven above;
Good intentions I had, but they melted away.
Now I grieve for the past; I am worthless and small.
My Lord! When the Judgement comes, what shall I say?

The Wind of Cognition raised passion in me[2];
To the suffering world my last tribute I pay.
Could this earth which amazes be ever replaced?
My Lord! When the Judgement comes, what shall I say?

On rich people

Rich people often treat each other, offering the best;
Tea with honey, buttered pancakes – nothing spared their guest.
But if a poor man, dressed in rags, should look upon their feast,
These noble Beys make fun of him and treat him like a beast[3].
But God will punish those who laugh and scoff at poverty.
Remember they might also find themselves in misery.
Our fancy Bey might be a dragon now, but bye and bye
The day could come when he is turned into a humble fly.
Just let him lose his satin clothes, and then without a clout
He'll find himself despised and by his family cast out.
And then he'll sicken, soon to die; his honour he won't save;
The worms will eat his rotting corpse in some obscure grave.
This life has shown us many such examples. So beware!
Refrain from money-grabbing and be happy with your share.
Remember to be humble and all arrogance eschew;
Among your fellow men make sure that you are always true.
And since you too must die one day, the riches from your trade,
The teas you drink, the food you eat will not come to your aid.

❖❖❖

---

2 Cognition: the Islamic mystical concept of *ma'rifāt*
3 Bey: Turkish *bey* or *beg*: 'Lord, master'. In Kazan Tatar, it later took the form *bay* – 'rich, noble'

The Russian Empire: 18th–19th Centuries

GABDERRAHIM ('ABDURRAHĪM) UTYZ IMYANI (1754–1836)

Gabderrahim ('Abdurrahīm) Utyz Imyany was born to a family of Islamic scholars near the present day city of Chistopol in Tatarstan. Having spent many years of his life in various parts of Central Asia and Afghanistan, he returned to his native village in 1789, where he taught in local schools. He died in Timash, his father's native village.

What it means to be a Jigit[1]

O proud and valiant horseman, sitting high upon your steed!
Display your virtues to your land and let it pay them heed.
If neighbours are in penury, then help them in their plight.
Your duty is unselfishness and doing what is right.

Make a promise and fulfil it; Faith you must obey.
Offending others for the slightest thing is not your way.
Let evil words not cross your lips; for liars have no use.
A simple smile conveys a perfect answer to abuse.

And do not boast that you are better than your fellow-men.
For beauty will not linger; it soon passes. And what then?
The most that you can hope for is a day or two, not more.
And then you'll rot and feed the worms. And that's the final score!

---

1 A brave young man, here, a 'knight'

For in this world are rich men and the poor whom they despise;
And fools as well dwell in our midst, and those whom we call wise;
If someone isn't master then he's but a servant's brat.
But common sense will tell us that it isn't quite like that.

One is crowned by fortune, and another's blessed by wit.
Whichever gift he's served by, he will be no worse for it.

Friendship

You have your home, but still the homeless you must not despise;
If people praise your wisdom, be not proud of being wise.

Enquire at times you do not know; in this there is no blame;
Denounce not others to increase the greatness of your name.

For ruin follows villainy, and surely you must know
That gossip and denunciation make your friend your foe.

If someone comes to you with rumours, entertain them never;
Bonds of friendship with a scoundrel you must firmly sever.

Gossip not yourself, and others' idle gossip shun,
By paying heed to empty prattle nothing will be won.

If you do good to someone in this life, you may be sure,
One day he will repay you for a kindness done before.

But if you practise evil, then the evil you create
Will bring you only sorrow and evoke an ill-starred fate.

If someone throws a stone at you, from angry thoughts refrain,
And opening your heart, with him good company maintain.

For in this century of ours which destiny betrayed
Only by the wise and brave is bad by good repaid.

Munajat[1]

Four things, my Lord, I ask of Thee:
The first — eternal Paradise;
And then esteem and sustenance;
The last is faith, which has no price.

Four things I ask Thee to reveal:
The first — a meeting with my love;
And offspring; then a houri; then
A slave in Paradise above.

And now, dear Allah, this I ask
That Thou shouldst four more gifts bestow:
First knowledge; then the will to work;
Then trust and safety I would know.

I now implore Thee in Thy grace,
From these four things deliver me:
From beggars and from sad mistrust;
From grief and doleful penury.

And when the Day of Judgement comes,
Unite me with the Righteous Four,
Siddiq, Faruq, Ali, Uthman[2],
Who stand for me by Heaven's door.

The four most sacred Holy Books:
The Taurat, the revered Injil[3],
The Psalms of David, the Quran —
Let them my broken spirit heal.

And in this world by Thee, oh Lord,
May we receive immunity
From accusation and arrest,
Anxiety and poverty.

---

1 munajat: a plea to Allah for spiritual prosperity
2 Siddiq (Abu Bakr), Faruq ('Umar), Uthman, 'Alī: the four 'Righteous Caliphs' who succeeded the Holy Prophet Muhammad
3 Taurat: The Old Testament; Injil — The New Testament

Upon the threshold of these four
I beg Thee, Lord, let me not stand:
A judge; a king who wears a crown;
A mufti[4] or a noble grand.

And may the evil of these four,
O Lord, for ever pass me by:
A spoilt man and an infidel;
The Devil and a cursed spy.

From these four ills, Most Bounteous Lord,
Throughout my life please keep me free:
From defamation's evil tongue;
From gossip, rumour, enmity.

Four limbs of mine, my Lord, I ask
That Thou shouldst in Thy wisdom spare,
And let them ever be with me:
My head, my tongue, my eye, my ear.

From 'Advice on the cleansing of the thoughts'

In earlier days, when I was young, I made
A journey to a land where Christians prayed.

I met a person; Grishka was his name,
The son of Kuz'ma; Christian all the same.

And with respect I asked to be his guest;
As evening fell we lay to take our rest.

My knowledge of the tongue he spoke was good,
And all he said I fully understood.

He spoke of faith, belief and righteous ways,
And to Islam he gave the utmost praise.

The Prophet's words, he said, seemed true and right;
His company found honour in his sight.

The doctrines of Islam had his respect
And in them he found nothing to reject.

---

4 Mufti: here, a Muslim lawyer

But in the faith he kept he found much blame
And said its faults gave many a cause for shame.

With several points and acts which formed his creed
He said that he profoundly disagreed.

He saw that Christians do much from their side
Which in good faith cannot be justified.

It seemed he disapproved of every rite
And ritual that was heinous in his sight.

But then the law of Islam touched his heart.
From his beliefs it seemed that he might part.

His eyes were full of tears when he was moved
To shun this faith of which he disapproved.

He had become a Muslim, I perceived.
At least he dared to say what he believed.

I rose to go outside; and he in turn
Arose with me and waited my return.

Such honour and respect he showed his guest.
That night I never closed my eyes in rest.

We fell to talking; every word of mine
Was welcomed and accepted as a sign.

Go seven times traversing land and sea;
You will not find a Muslim true as he.

By dawn we were exhausted in our search.
Just then a bell chimed from a nearby church.

The bell rang out and filled the air with sound,
And Christians flocked to make their daily round.

Then Grishka raised himself up from the floor,
And putting on his belt stepped to the door.

'At such an hour', I said, ' where do you go?'
He answered: 'That, my friend, you surely know.

The bells ring out, and they direct the way,
And tell us that the time has come to pray.'

I said: 'But this is not your way . . . you see,
You surely are a Muslim just like me.'

He answered; 'So much weighs upon my heart.
But from my faith could I be torn apart?

We are so used to our old Christian ways.
Disgrace will surely follow him who strays.

The habits of a lifetime cling so fast;
Our faith, for good or ill, will always last.

My friends and kin will cover me with blame;
They will revile and curse me in my shame.

Perhaps we stumbled on the path we trod,
And we were left in darkness by our God.

And of His mercy we shall be bereft;
Like infidels disgraced we shall be left.

To you the Lord Almighty has been kind;
He granted you Islam to keep and mind.

Give thanks to Allah for Islam, and pray
That you, like us, will never go astray'.

Whoever tries the door that is forbidden
Will be assailed by all that should be hidden

So Grishka took the path of sad disgrace
And from Islam forever turned his face.

From 'The gifts of time'

When travel lost its charm, I ceased to roam,
And came to settle in my native home.

How glad the heart is when the journey ends;
How good to meet your family and your friends.

My re-appearance gave them much surprise;
And many things I saw amazed my eyes.

In turbans sat the wise for consultation,
And from their lips streamed mystic revelation.

Their talk on faith and custom was so free;
So blissful was their joy in ecstasy.

The call to prayer rang out; they made their way
In masses to the mosque to kneel and pray.

When I beheld their piety, my heart
Was gladdened and I hastened to take part.

A pious year I spent with great delight.
But then I felt not everything was right.

With every passing day it seemed more clear
That piety was superficial here.

I taxed them on the law and saw at once
There is no point in talking to a dunce.

On lore and custom they were quite confused;
Essential and permitted were misused.

Their knowledge was quite shallow; they were fools.
Much more like children, careless of the rules.

Their minds deflected from the righteous way;
They could not see how they had gone astray.

The dust of ignorance obscured their sight.
In vain I tried to bring them to the light.

Far better not to mix with them, my friend.
Their poisonous thoughts will bring about your end.

And no reproach you make can change a thing;
To lawless customs they so fondly cling.

By them Islam is poorly understood.
They do not even know how to be good.

One dons a robe and claims to be a shaikh;
But you can see at once he is a fake.

They learn the words of mystics off by heart
Deception has become their finest art.

Rich offerings and gifts are their main aim;
Their piety is sham; their wisdom lame.

Unable to distinguish right from wrong,
They still preach homilies the whole day long.

Their grasp of mysticism is unsound;
Their horses' feet are firmly on the ground.

They find their followers by trick and stealth,
With one sole aim – to take away their wealth.

And many fools are captured by their spell.
How sleek they are! No wonder they do well.

ABELMANIKH KARGALY (1782–1833?)

Abelmanikh Kargaly was born in the Tatar settlement of Kargaly near Orenburg. After studying in the local madrasa, *which had acquired a high reputation, he travelled to Bukhara, where he furthered his education in the madrasa of Niyaz Koly Turkmani. From 1816, he travelled to Turkey and visited other parts of the Middle East. On his return to his native land, despite his erudition, he became a farmer. His last poem is dated 1833. After this, he made a pilgrimage to Mecca, during which he seems to have died. Abelmanikh's verse is strongly influenced by that of the Sufis.*

A wasted life

Now, Manikh, you have reached the age of forty;
Your youth was wasted in the frivolous quest
For earthly beauty. All your glorious summers
And winters too were vainly laid to rest.

And in your spring you failed to sow your harvest;
Your autumn yielded nothing much at all.
The sword of God hangs o'er your head and threatens.
Do you not fear that one day it might fall?

My poor one! Will you leave the world so tainted,
Corrupt and bad, a Muslim just in name?
Deceived by worldly pleasures? This was written
By destiny. But is your fate to blame?

If you believe the promises of Islam,
Of resurrection on the Final Day,
You must prepare and give yourself to Allah.
Each day and night joined in the Holy Fray.

Ignorance

How long will this soul in the body remain as a guest?
   I did not know.

My life is now over; this world was a miserable test.
   I did not know.

Fine towers of ignorance I once built up in my heart,
But see! They are shattered and now they lie broken apart.
   I did not know.

By dreams I was charmed, and at night I neglected my prayer.
The one who is wakeful will rule and be given his share.
   I did not know.

I could not recite as the pious and faithful ones can;
The greatest authority given us is the Quran.
   I did not know.

And all I accomplished in life I accomplished in vain,
But only through righteousness can we find spiritual gain.
   I did not know.

HIBATULLAH SALIKHOV (1794–1867)

Hibatullah Salikhov was born in the Orenburg district of Russia, where many exiled Tatars had settled. He studied at the famous madrasa of Kargala, but in his youth was sent to work in the Siberian salt mines. Little else is know of his life. His work was printed in Kazan in 1856.

A tale with a moral

Some time ago I heard a tale at which I laughed;
So hear it now, my friends; its really not so daft.

Two fools went for a walk; the road was not the best.
They walked and walked so long, and then resolved to rest.

One said: 'You have a sleep, and I'll watch through the night;
No need for foolish fears; my friendship isn't slight.

'In time, we'll change the watch; I'll sleep, you'll be awake;
And if a foe should come, I'll fight him for your sake.

'No mercy shall I spare; his very life I'll take.'
So one went off to sleep; the other stayed awake.

He watched on all four sides, but nothing did he spy,
When suddenly a snake with stealth came creeping by.

It hardly left a trace upon the grass that night.
The watchman froze and thought: 'I wonder, will it bite?'

'Now will it bite or not? My task is not in vain.
If it decides to bite, I'll see that it is slain.'

The snake drew near; the friend was very fast asleep.
Uncovering its fangs it now prepared to leap.

But then it saw the guard poised ready for the fray,
And thought: 'He'll have my life. Best take myself away.

'For if I hang around, he'll kill me. That's for sure.'
The snake slipped off; the fool stayed watching as before.

Content, he looked about – a watchman well in place;
Then suddenly he saw upon his dear friend's face –

Not just upon his face, but there upon eyes
Had settled a great swarm, at least a hundred flies.

The watchman was put out, for flies were in the end
Accursed foes which caused great suffering to his friend.

So thereupon, the guard in a responsive tone
Vowed vengeance on the flies, and chose a hefty stone.

And taking careful aim he raised it to the sky;
The stone came thudding down and put out his friend's eye.

The other grabbed his knife, for could he really know,
When being half asleep, who was his friend or foe?

He knocked the watchmen down, and with blood-curdling cries,
Attacked him in blind rage and took out both his eyes.

Then hurriedly he traced the way that he had come,
Forgetting all his plans, and soon arrived back home.

From home he went to court: 'Give judgement, Qazi! See!
I've lost an eye. Just look and give redress to me.

'My friend left me for dead.' The judge gave careful thought;
In sympathy he said: 'The culprit must be sought,

'And have his eye knocked out in answer to your plea.'
His constables all ran to serve this just decree.

They brought the guilty one to answer to the case.
The fool was in the dock without his eyes in place.

From head to foot in blood he stood before the court.
'Now answer to the charge!' He said just what he thought:

'My friend was fast asleep and I was standing guard.
His enemies I fought when they fell on him hard.

'For that he took my sight. Now judge, can that be fair?
And then he ran away. I really don't know where.

Considering the case, the judges of the court
Were angry and cried out: 'The plaintiff must be brought

'And given punishment. His eye must be torn out.
In darkness must he dwell. The case is quite borne out.'

Then summing up the fools, they ordered that their kin
Should be informed at once and forced to take them in.

◆◆◆

How did you find this tale? Not bad as stories go.
But have you grasped the point? I'd really like to know.

The watchman saw the snake but didn't kill the beast.
A snake's an enemy. That we agree at least.

Its poisoned fangs deal death. He spared his enemy.
Perhaps his friend's dear life was not so dear. We'll see.

In dire necessity his reason did not serve,
But when he saw a fly he found he had more nerve.

Then boiling up with rage, and malice in his eyes,
He couldn't fathom which were eyes and which were flies!

Thing's can't get out of hand like this. And in the end.
Who was the bigger fool? The watchman or his friend?

The latter gouged two eyes, and leaping with a cry,
Rushed off to tell the judge, then lost his own good eye.

He did it by himself, and hoped to fix the blame.
But many people here are really just the same.

No need to doubt; a bit of sense is all it takes.
The leaders of our land remind us all of snakes.

Like snakes they too wear scales, rubbed up and shined,
And they can be the death of you, if they've a mind.

For if by chance you make – God save us with all speed! –
A minimal mistake in thought or word or deed,

This error they'll construe as 'malice by design',
And just for this they'll have your head upon the line.

Then they'll investigate; a pile of books they'll read;
To every subtle hint they'll pay the greatest heed.

And they'll exaggerate and swear that dust is earth,
Abusing all the world and cursing every birth.

No friends for the aggrieved. You will not see a soul.
A dinar's what they want, and that's their only goal.

And if this cherished gift falls straight into their hands:
'More dinars and dirhams!' Demands upon demands!

The cause of this affront is not your actual crime,
For there are always ways of stopping tongues in time.

And even if your guilt is deeper than the skies,
A gift will be enough to make them shut their eyes.

There's nothing like a gift to cloud a prying glance.
If someone's crime is bad, they'll take a harsher stance.

They'll ask for much more gold, the most he can procure,
And then they'll let him off – the purest of the pure!

But if he has no gold to give and cannot pay,
But wants to save himself as quickly as he may,

They'll confiscate his horse and offer him instead
Safe conduct on the road wherever he is led.

They'll usher him along and gently point the way
To anywhere so long as it's quite far away.

But if they're faced themselves with similar demands,
Or ordered by the Shah to jump to his commands,

Or sort out some dark deed, at once they'll go around
And visit any house where riches might be found.

Then taxes are imposed; they never cease to rise,
While they sit swilling wine, up to their necks in lies!

GABDELJABBAR ('ABDUL JABBĀR) KANDALY (1797–1860)

Gabdeljabbar ('Abdul Jabbār) Kandaly was born in the Samara district of Russia, and studied in various madrasas and schools in the Volga region. There he mastered Russian and several local languages. Little is known of his life except that he taught in various madrasas and spent some time in prison. His stubbornness and irascibility seem to have earned him many enemies. In his verse he is frequently scathing about his society and contemporaries.

The mulla and his wife

Dressed up in your fur overcoat of radiant yellow hue,
Respected Mulla, out you go to eat, and your wife too.

You have the place of honour there, and by you sits your wife;
You stuff your mouths with food, and praise the Lord for this good life.

You thrust yourself upon your host; the peasant wasn't mean;
For you he made a fatty soup, and carved a chicken clean.

Now don't be shy, dear Mulla; every chance you have to seize;
Your belly has no bottom. Come and fill it at your ease.

Lap up your soup, and finish off the chicken. Never spare
The cups of wine; enjoy your tea and cake without a care.

You'll sing, you'll drink, from the Quran you'll read a sacred verse;
An extra little kopeck will not overload your purse.

But, Hazrat Mulla[1]! Watch your step; take measure of the game.
The peasants will cool off; you'll find that things aren't quite the same.

No sizzling pancakes for you now; the crocks no longer clatter;
And not a scrap of halva[2]; and no money for your patter.

Your wife will moan: 'What is there not a single invitation?'
She'll beat you with her felt-lined boot in her exasperation.

---

1 Hazrat Mulla: 'Lord Mulla!'. The Arabic title of respect, *hazrat*, is here, of course, used somewhat ironically
2 halva: a sticky sweet dish common in Muslim countries, as well as in Russia

Somehow you'll make ablutions, and you'll rush to say your prayer,
Remembering those bygone days that are no longer there.

You used to ride upon the peasants' backs, your wife and you;
You scoffed their chickens and their geese, devoured their
    turkeys too.

A chicken dreams of millet, and a stray dog of a bone;
So you will dream that you're invited not to eat alone.

'Dear wife!', you'll cry. 'An invitation! Supper for tonight!'
And in your sleep you'll eat your fill. Rave on, you parasite!

Your boots of felt have frozen and like skis they slip and slide.
Dear Mulla! With your wife you've put on weight and lost your
    pride.

To get free meals from house to house you'll traipse, and all
    your life
You'll fill your bellies shamelessly, o Mulla with your wife!

From 'Sahibjamal'[1]

For you I prayed; for you my thoughts were meant,
Absorbed in fervent prayer, I drew so near.
The words I spoke I clothed in tender verse
That one day my entreaty you might hear.

O crystal of the rarest form, my love!
Sahibjamal, the sweetest and the best!
For you I lost my reason and my mind;
For you I sacrificed my peace and rest.

Why do you hide yourself away, my dream?
Your words I long to hear, your own sweet voice.
Allow the pearls to drop from your dear mouth,
That in your charming speech I may rejoice.

I might compare you to a golden fruit;
The vision of your beauty burns my heart.
But I grow tired; I have no strength to bear
The yoke of our remaining far apart.

❖❖❖

---

1 Sahibjamal: Persian *sahib-jamāl* 'The Beautiful One'; here, the name of the poet's beloved

My dazzling treasure of the purest gold!
A beauty rare as yours I have not found
Nor in the villages remote and still,
Nor in the city full of noise and sound.

Your fascination haunts me at this hour;
Your magic spell has robbed my eyes of sight.
I swear by the Almighty that my tale
Is far from rumour born of gossip light.

Amongst the dwellers of Parau[2] your charm
Has captured every heart. How people long
To catch your glance which blinds them with its flash,
To hear your words that stream into a song!

For only Paradise could cherish you;
Your knife has pierced my heart with its bare blade.
You are the wind that roams the distant steppe,
The morning breeze that blows through vale and glade.

Because of you and for you on the paths
Of grieving and of sorrow have I stepped;
Amid the thorns and burrs I used to walk
To your Parau, and as I walked I wept.

Why are you colder than the driven snow?
How could my heart have borne such painful days?
No! May your beauty fling around the world
A girdle, and its glory shine and daze!

The tale of how I burn for you in vain,
Of how I give my life to you each day —
Let it be told in every place on earth!
Let every clime hear what I write and say!

All know that I have no more shame or pride;
All see the snares and tangles I have laid.
Until the Day of Judgement comes at last
May this remain and from the world not fade.

Sahibjamal, now distant, you decay,
But you remain the word for beauty yet;
The sound of your sweet name still echoes forth;
Your comely features no one will forget.

---

2 Parau: a Tatar village

You silly child! Why can you not believe
The tale of springtime love, the broken heart,
The sad beloved locked in her own land,
The lover in his country torn apart?

They see each other only through their dreams
And wait impatiently as darkness falls;
They pine for one another constantly;
One spirit to the other spirit calls.

But these two distant limits are our own.
You are my heart and soul, and this you know.
How many schemes and plans do you conceal
As you keep silence in the winter snow?

Will you at least accept my kind advice?
Do not debase yourself and waste your life.
A dull and oafish husband has no thoughts.
Of some poor peasant would you be a wife?

In summer and in winter you will toil
Day in day out; the seasons will pass by.
And as your life grows shorter with your grief
The heart within your breast will fade and die.

And with your sickle you will reap the corn,
A ragged scarf tied loosely round your head.
The thorns will scratch, the blood flow from your hands;
In cornfields burrs and thistles make their bed.

And as you labour you will sweat; the earth
Will take the moisture pouring down your thighs.
And from disease like stubble you will fall;
In burning fever you will heave your sighs.

If to a peasant once you give your hand,
Your future life will be a vale of tears;
The yoke of misery placed round your neck
Will take the freedom of your former years.

The lord who owns the land is cruel and harsh;
The life of serfs in slavery is spent.
A peasant hardly has five kopecks left,
When he has paid and parted with the rent.

In common sandals you will trudge along
The muddy roads and face eternal fear.
At last, reduced to ashes, you will live,
And shame will be the death of you, my dear.

And this will be the sum of your whole life,
For misery in labour sows its seed.
At times your hunger pangs will seem so harsh;
At every moment you will be in need.

A fisherman, they say, has just two things:
An empty stomach and a wet behind.
But every day he goes down to his stream,
And this time hopes that Fortune will be kind.

❖❖❖

I dreamed that I was in the place you live
And there I shot a bird. You ask me why?
Because of my beloved I have lost
The peace which I enjoyed in times gone by.

Whatever age they are, all people drink
And eat, as if no grief assails their heart.
The whole world has grown wearisome for me;
I crave no food or drink, but lie apart.

And then I thought that I might come to you;
Perhaps a chance encounter on the way;
And I might take you off in my embrace.
In dreams I hold creation in my sway.

But no! In vain I tramped the dusty roads;
I wrote and prayed. 'The goal lies far ahead,
And all is unattainable, you fool!
Your wandering is useless.' This I said.

My reason now is overcome by tears,
And darkness shrouds the destiny I sought.
My darling, there is no straight path to you.
I travelled, but alas! returned with nought.

GALI ('ALĪ) CHOKRI (1826–1889)

Gali Chokry was born in the Ufa district, where his father worked as a farmer. Having received his education at a village madrasa, he began to teach in various schools in the Kazan area from 1849. Locally he gained the reputation of being an Islamic scholar and performed the pilgrimage to Mecca three times. He was also known for his powers of healing and hypnosis and was once accused of being a sorcerer.

The sacking of Bolgar

A wondrous city, grey from years and age
Which vied in beauty with Kazan, the Fair,
Bolgar, the holy refuge of Islam,
Now lies in ruins; nothing else is there.

Built high upon the most imposing site,
It could be seen from every place around.
How fine and proud its minarets and mosques!
But of them now can little trace be found.

Bolgar, the mighty fortress of the Khans;
Bashkir[1] the city was, it was Tatar.
It viewed the rolling planes from its great heights
And welcomed young and old from near and far.

Its books and letters in the past were famed;
Its scholars were renowned for skill and grace.
Within its ancient borders Muslims dwelt,
And here Islam was given pride of place.

Then Timur came, his black and villain horde
Slew children, and the old were beaten down.
To crush the Muslims was his evil plan;
He longed to bring destruction to the town.

He stormed in like a fire from the steppe;
His blows engulfed the city walls in flame.
Bolgar was laid to waste, its buildings razed.
How many men and women died in shame.

---

1 Bashkir: a Turkic people, whose language is closely related to Tatar. Their country, Bashkortostan, borders on the Republic of Tatarstan

With sword and fire the enemy drove through
And cannon balls fell from the air like rain;
The clash of steel rang out in every street.
The city lay in ruins, racked with pain.

Ah, robber! How your army was despised!
To ashes you reduced Bolgar, the Fair,
The sanctuary where, by the grace of God,
The innocent and sinless might repair.

O murderer! These cloisters of good works,
How could you dare to touch them with your blow,
Condemning all who dwelt in them to tears?
And to their sorry lot fell grief and woe.

Then honour was accorded to the foe.
All feared the demon who would not relent
From carnage. He made merry as they died.
At last before him every neck was bent.

He drove the people to the barren wastes;
He drove them from the river to the sands,
To salty marshes where no grass could grow,
To waterless abodes and desert lands.

The men he slew, but women and young girls
He made them captives, sparing their sad life.
Bolgar was burnt by this black-hearted foe.
From then began the age of pain and strife.

The ones who lived went grieving far away,
Recalling their dear home and happier times;
In dust and ashes now they shed their tears,
While wandering through the sands of foreign climes.

In praise of Kazan

In fair Kazan they make all kinds of shoes;
Their gowns and scarves are quite beyond compare;
And experts praise the goods which they produce,
While all agree their talents are most rare. The handicrafts of women are first class;
Their needlework attracts much adulation.
The number of the skull-caps in this town
Is equal to the sum of all creation.

The houses and the buildings are so clean;
The men and women living there so neat;
The strains of purest singing fills the air,
A mine of perfect knowledge every street.

So many doctors, singers, learned men;
So many writers ready to amaze.
Ah, blessed refuge of this splendid world!
All men in every clime will sing your praise.

How wonderful the sermons that are preached;
The shaikhs outnumber forests in Kazan.
The voices of the clerics ring out clear,
As they intone the Glorious Quran.

And in this land of Bulgar you might find
So many cities that are rich and rare,
But with the great attractions of Kazan
No other town or city could compare.

Lines on his own verse

Dear Gali! When they show your limping verse
To critics who are always harsh and terse,
They will exclaim: 'Please take away this screed!
It's rubbish, not the thing we like to read!'

But to my friends quite frankly I reply:
'They begged me write them, and so I comply.
With all my strength I've laboured as I should,
And given to the people what I could.'

YAKOV YEMELYANOV (1848–1893)

Yakov Yemelyanov was born in Kazan to a family of Christian Orthodox Tatars. After his education in a Russian College, he became a priest, but because of his Tatar background he was frequently obliged to change his place of work. For much of his life he taught in Tatar schools in the Kazan district.

Grief

Let grief not come and stand before me;
Let it from my world depart.
With its icy, pressing tempest
May it never shake my heart.

Nor let groaning shake my spirit;
Firm as a rock it stands in me;
Let it store within its vessel
All the trials of misery.

Its will grows firm within that vessel.
See how proud it is to know
That fortune's hand can never break it,
Bend it with its pain and woe.

For rather grief is bent before it;
Let misfortune step aside.
On land and sea my heart grows stronger;
Everywhere it is well tried.

Well tried, and stronger than disaster;
Not like a wilting stem at all,
Every storm it rides with courage;
In alarm it will not fall.

It will not fall my living spirit,
Never burnt by evil's brand.
Ah Grief! When you tried to confront it,
You fell down and could not stand.

Yes, Grief! You fell. There is no ardour
In the malice of your fire.
Though in my breast you boil with vigour,
To crush me you cannot aspire.

A poor life

Well, today it's the fifth, and quite early
I rose in the usual way.
I went through my pockets. They're empty.
All gone with the wind, as they say!

So taking some rags from my cupboard,
I went to the pawnbroker's place.
But he wouldn't give me a kopeck.
I returned with a miserable face.

If my eyes hadn't dried up completely,
I might have shed tears. But I'd told
The old woman to heat up some water
For tea, when my rags had been sold.

The samovar gleamed with its copper,
But vainly it sang down the street.
We'd got tea from the neighbours, but sugar
Was lacking. Another defeat!

So we put out the fire to save fuel
(Conserving resources is best).
And decided to wait for tomorrow,
And let the poor samovar rest.

It slowly grew dark, and quite strangely
The moon didn't rise in the sky.
So to give her some light for the cooking
My wife lit a spill and stood by.

On the stove she had boiled some potatoes,
And shedding a bit of tear,
Pathetically said (how it touched me!):
'Take the ones that are soundest, my dear.'

The innermost depths of my spirit
Were touched by her pitiful tone,
And I realised as soon as I heard it
That the old lady's grief was my own.

'No, I'm full, wife', I said to console her.
From my voice it was easy to tell
That we hadn't got even a tea-leaf,
And like her I was crying as well.

So in silence we bore our misfortune;
Lying down in that silence so deep,
We covered ourselves with a mangy fur-coat
In case we should freeze in our sleep.

Slander

Abide by the law,
Commune with the saints,
Be just and fair – you name it.
But even though
Your conscience is clear,
Slander will come to defame it.

Be silent and suffer,
Shout or groan,
Make heavy of grief, take it lightly;
Conceal your thoughts
Stop up their mouths;
Slander will cling to you tightly.

Go out of the town,
Move off to the sticks,
Leave cold or heat behind you;
From mountain to sea
Keep shifting your place;
Slander will always find you.

You can stay in the house
Or go out in the street
Or cover you head and be wily;
Shut up the gates
And lock up the doors;
Slander will wriggle in slyly.

Horrible, awful
It hovers around
Like a flock of black crows to annoy us;
Try to drive it away,
Lose your mind and shout out;
Slander will always destroy us.

Arrogance

Take all the weapons of the world
To fight with arrogance. And then
Tie it down with chains of brass
So it may never rise again.

And let those heavy chains of brass
Weigh down and bind it to the ground.
And let all men spit on its face
With loathing as they pass around.

Yes let them spit, so it may know
How vile it is and how we hate
Its very being; from the earth
All traces we'll eradicate.

And not one shadow will remain;
Its shade like ghostly smoke will flee.
The source of all disgrace abates,
Condemned by its own infamy.

GABDULLA ('ABDULLĀH) TUKAI (1886-1913)

Gabdulla ('Abdullāh) Tukai was born in the small village of Kushlauch in the Kazan district. Orphaned while still very young, he was fostered by several families, and after studying in local madrasas, he became a printer and journalist. His verse received great acclaim, and during his lifetime he was recognised as one of the foremost Tatar writers. He never had a home of his own and lived in various hotels in Kazan. He died of tuberculosis at the age of 26. His grave is now a national memorial, and the centenary of his birth was celebrated by UNESCO in 1986.

The Haymarket[1]

I

Now let's begin this tale with Karakhmet[2];
And people may think kindly of us yet!

Or should we go and see what's over there?
Nikitin's horses at the circus fair[3].

Here in Kazan praiseworthy deeds abound,
But sights like this are rarely to be found.

What God ordains will come to pass in truth;
And so Nikitin opened up his booth.

The glorious Circus has a Muslim fighter,
A sturdy, brave young man – there's no one brighter.

As powerful as Zarkum or Salsal;
More wily than the great Sa'it Battal[4].

A story comes to mind; now let's be bold
And find the way the story should be told.

Let grocers, butchers, tanners be amazed
And candle-makers, butter-churners dazed!

---

1 Haymarket: The Sennoi Bazaar of Kazan. The poem, a parody of the medieval work Kisek-Bash, 'The Severed Head', was written in 1908. For Tukai, the Kisek-Bash, which served as a religious text-book in Muslim schools, was a symbol of backwardness and religious fanaticism
2 Karakhmet: a celebrated circus wrestler, whose exploits inspired the nationalistic and religious sentiments of the Tatar petty-bourgeoisie
3 Nikitin: the owner of the Kazan circus, known in Kazan as Konnaya Komed' or 'Horse Comedy'
4 Zarkum, Salsal, Sa'it Battal: heroes of various Islam folk literatures

There, in the Haymarket, one fruitful day
I found a theme. My story's on its way.

A fine bazaar! From dawn to dusk the noise
Of cunning traders and the market boys.

They rush upon the stalls; they shout and haggle
Our simpletons and rascals in a gaggle.

For centuries this great bazaar's well known –
A place where everyone looks to his own.

So sudden, like a dust-storm, stumbling, gushing
To Unbelievers' Corner all came rushing[5];

'O Muslims! Tell us what you're running for.
A fire? An earthquake? Not a Holy War?'

I also followed as the crowd went teeming
To Moscow Street, and thought: 'Can I be dreaming?'

There on the tarmac, like a huge round stone,
A human head was rolling all alone.

So fast it was determined to proceed,
It passed a tramcar coming at full speed.

The Miracle sped on to Godless Gate,
And stopped where idlers often congregate.

They looked. Indeed it was a human head,
Cut off, but still alive. That's what they said.

It had no trunk, but tears streamed from its eyes.
No doubt a martyr. See the way it sighs!

A Kafir's sword had cut it at its peak.
But look! Its tongue still moves and it can speak.

Its beard is still well-trimmed and snowy white;
And from its brow there shines a dazzling light.

It beats itself upon the dusty ground.
Lord Ali would have wept to hear the sound.

---

5 Unbelievers' Corner: a street corner near the Haymarket Mosque, the meeting place in Kazan of religious fanatics who supported traditional methods of education

A pang of grieving overwhelmed the throng:
'Ah Hapless Head! To whom didst thou belong?'

They all wept tears. Oh how the sight appals!
The frenzied fezzes jumped down from their stalls.

The fresh tanned pelts, which lay there in the sun
Were trampled as they wailed: 'Oh Luckless One!'

The sacks of flour were mourning for the dead;
A beggar woman screamed before the Head:

'How not to weep? All speech has lost its powers.
The Head's religion was the same as ours.'

The Severed Head prolonged its bitter lay;
The old men asked it: 'What befell thee? Say!'

With bitter glances, turning to their side,
So dolefully the Severed Head replied:

'Now pay attention to this tale of mine;
My pilgrimages numbered ninety-nine.

I visited Hejaz; I swear I've been
To Jeddah, Mecca, Yemen – these I've seen.

As councillor of the Duma I have served;
For me alone that honour was reserved,

And when I traded wares from Moscow, then
My profit always stood at nine to ten.

I read the Holy Book when day was done,
And fifteen wives I married one by one.

At night I saw the ladies of the town;
By day I was a person of renown.

My last wife gave to me my greatest boon –
A lovely boy, as radiant as the moon.

They are no longer here, and hence my tears;
The only joys of my declining years.

One night they were abducted by a Dev.
Now as a Muslim your kind help I crave.

He hid them in the bottom of a well;
Since then I've had no sleep. This you can tell.

If you will not assist me to retrieve
My wife and son, I'll curse you without leave!

II

The old men took their counsel wise and true
And said: 'No point in moaning. What to do?

Let's ask the Tsar for soldiers in his pay,
And let them shoot the Dev without delay.

Or rather send Maksudi on a mission.
Just let the Duma deal with his submission[6].

We voted for him at the State Election;
He surely owes us much for our selection.

Or call the Holy *Ishan* with his lash[7].
He'll make the monster squirm for being rash.'

Then one of them, an Aksakal[8], announced:
'I know the way to have the monster trounced.

But for our task we need young Karakhmet.
He's got the strength, and he's our safest bet.

He'll fight his best and leave the Dev for dead,
And get the boy back for the Severed Head,'

The whole bazaar erupted: 'Karakhmet!
Good fellow! That's the best idea yet!'

May Allah give him strength! Yes, he's our choice!'
Then someone from the people raised his voice:

'Eh, Minlebai! Go now, do as we say.'
He stamped his boots and ran without delay.

---

6 Maksudi Sadri: a famous Tatar politician, deputy of the Duma, the Russian Parliament, who went into exile after the October Revolution of 1917
7 Ishan with his Lash: a Muslim spiritual leader in Kazan who is said to have been able to cure the sick with his lash
8 Aksakal: 'white beard', in Tatar, an old man

Then Karakhmet, the man of do or die,
Arrived there in the twinkling of an eye.

Before the folk about his task he sped
And in his hands he took the Severed Head.

But when he tried to lift it, he soon found
He couldn't even raise it from the ground.

Ah, what a sorry sight, poor Karakhmet!
He snorted as he broke out in a sweat.

The Head exclaimed: 'He's gone out of his mind.
He thought that he could do the task assigned.

But let a thousand like him now be brought;
Medvyedev, even Zaikin could be sought[9];

This feat would be so far beyond their power.
Don't talk to me about it at this hour.

Fanaticism weighs upon their brain;
Attempts to lift that up are all in vain;

And stubbornness within their storehouse crowds;
Like beery steam it hangs in heavy clouds.

In wagon loads the dullness of their mind
With empty self-importance is enshrined.

They think that only what is old is holy,
And what is new is infidel and lowly.'

III

'Ah, such a saintly Head!' the crowd averred.
'But it no longer holds its place conferred.'

They milled around the Head and mobbed the fighter.
With charity their hearts became much lighter.

Our Hercules, his hair on end, arose;
He breathed the fire of anger from his nose:

---

9 Medvyedev, Zaikin: famous circus wrestlers of pre-revolutionary Russia

'I may not live, but if my life I save,
I will succeed and slay the evil Dev.

Whatever happens, till my future's brighter,
The Circus will not see Nikitin's fighter.

My luck runs out, but till I seal my fate,
Let Zaikin, Pugachov and others wait.

I shall behead the Dev, or else I'll perish.
I mean to win. May God these fond hopes cherish.'

'May fortune aid you!', cried the whole bazaar;
'Help him who is a Muslim as we are.'

'I must depart', he shouted. 'No delay!
Where all have failed, I'll surely find the way.'

And when he heard this oath, the Severed Head
Began to beam, and in his weakness said:

'O Giant! Please accept my gratitude;
For in your hands lies my decrepitude.

Renounce your freedom and your friendships here,
And take this blessing to allay your fear.

Good men, cry after me as I proceed:
"May Karakhmet have victory in his deed!"'

The hands of young and old rose to the sky;
The whole bazaar erupted with the cry:

'Great God Almighty! Prosper Karakhmet!
With strength may he complete his journey yet.'

They dropped their hands, and suddenly with a wham
Right on the corner there appeared a tram.

So Karakhmet jumped on without delay,
And bought a ticket, full return, two-way.

The people saw the giant off and cried:
May God protect him on his holy ride!'

The tram flew like the wind. Ah what a race!
The Head rolled on beside it keeping pace.

Then all at once, as if to lend their help,
The butchers' dogs came running with a yelp.

At this some stupid people sneered and said:
'These curly-tails can't catch you, Severed Head.'

A feathered arrow, nay, a racing horse.
The tram passed Godless Corner in its course,

And clanking on the rails the tramcar sped,
While boys threw pebbles at the Severed Head.

The City Book Shop flashed by on the right;
The press of *Al-Islah* came into sight[10].

Krestovnikov's great factory[11] on their way
Passed from their view, and day merged into day.

For six whole days they travelled without care,
Until they reached a wasteland, grim and bare.

The tramcar reached its final terminus;
The Head rolled on a little past the bus.

'Have we arrived? Please tell me where we are',
Said Karakhmet still sitting in the car.

'Yes, get down quickly', cried the Head. 'Alight.
The goal of our desire is now in sight.

From here you go on foot, my valiant man,
And you will see the great Lake of Kaban.

A magic well lies in the murky creek,
And in its depths there dwells the Dev we seek.

IV

Now while we're here, let's have a little break
And learn about the mysteries of the Lake.

Its waters cover wonders known of old:
Bronze villages and cities made of gold.

---

10 Al-Islāh: 'The Reform', a progressive Tatar newspaper published from Kazan between 1907–1917
11 A famous soap factory in Kazan

The deer have marble horns, and I could tell
Of its six-hundred-headed snakes as well.

A wicked black-faced water-sprite lives there
And steals a little girl or boy each year.

And when the army of the Tsar arrived
From Moscow with its cannon, and contrived

To take Kazan, the Khans took all their treasure
And hurled it in the water for good measure.

The depths engulfed their riches, so they say;
And there was nothing left to take away.

In that deep Lake, it's generally recounted,
Lies silver, gold and wealth that can't be counted.

It's said one day the waters will recede;
But that's just to excite the people's greed.

That day will come when all life's joy is taught
In Muslim schools where knowledge must be sought.

Then all will glean the fruits the water yields;
No work required to reap these fertile fields!

The years go by; the waters might abate
As by the Lake the Muslim faithful wait.

V

But while they're waiting, let's pick up our thread,
And see what's happened to the Severed Head.

Six thousand coils of rope brave Karakhmet
Unwound from his wide girth; now he was set.

The free end of the rope he deftly tied
Around the Head's huge tongue; the poor Head sighed.

He crashed into the Lake and clutched the rope;
Then found the Dev's deep well, now full of hope.

Day follows day in this abysmal flight;
Our hero loses track of day and night.

By turning cartwheels, see how he descends;
The old saint, Khizr[12], his noble cause befriends.

He prays to Allah; down and down he creeps;
Upon the bank the Head in anguish weeps.

In this descent ten gruelling days were passed;
The bottom of the well was reached at last.

The world around him dimmed; his sight grew blind,
But Karakhmet soon focussed his sharp mind.

Within a trice he opened his bright eyes,
And saw a palace there of wondrous size.

Ibrai of old Kasimov[13] would have been
Amazed at such a sight by him unseen.

Above its gates a dark green board was hung,
And with these haughty words it grimly swung:

*The Muslim Evildoers' Holy Order
As Founded by Gainan, the Pious Warder*[14].

Towards himself our hero pulled the gate
And went in boldly, for he could not wait.

In front of him a peasant-woman knelt,
Enough to cause the hardest heart to melt.

Her countenance makes all the world seem bright;
Her saintly kindness drives away the night.

She bows in humble prayer; each time a sigh,
So lightly uttered, speeds towards the sky.

And at her feet the pool of tears she's shed.
She is the woman of the Severed Head.

Now Karakhmet makes for the second hall;
He shields his eyes; its dreadful sights appal.

---

12 Khizr: a Muslim saint who is regarded as the patron of travellers. Khizr is said to have accompanied Alexander the Great on his quest for the Water of Eternal Life. Having drunk from the spring, he attained immortality
13 Ibrai of Kasimov: a merchant known for his excesses and bad end
14 Gainan Vaisov: the founder of a nationalistic religious sect known as 'The Holy Regiment'

Five-hundred True Believers! See their pains!
Their hands and feet all bound in iron chains.

'Protect us, Powerful Lord! Don't let us die!
Have mercy, O Bagautdin[15]!' They cry.

They scream like madmen, roll around the place;
And each one has a crazed and frenzied face.

Poor things! They see the fighter. How they squeal!
And to his conscience how they make appeal!

'Our life is hard. Have mercy. Don't forget!
Go crush the evil monster, Karakhmet!

We numbered thousands last year in the fall,
But now we are five-hundred, and that's all!'

At last into a hall our hero sped;
He found the monster fast asleep in bed.

His dome-like head was bigger than a crate;
The hat he wore could hardly fit his pate.

Above his lip a thick moustache that trails
As greasy and disgusting as rats' tails.

Each finger like a man in form and size;
He's gorged on Tatar blood. That's how he lies.

Now Karakhmet is bold. That we all know.
'Still sleeping?', he cries out and prods his foe.

'Wake up!' He kicks the Dev who's lying there;
The monster sleeps and doesn't turn a hair.

Another kick; at this the monster groans;
His blazing eyes half open as he moans.

Still wondering where he is, he looks around;
He curses and blasphemes – an awful sound:

'And why have you come here without permission
To spoil my rest and treat me with derision?

---

15 Bagautdin Vaisov, the father of Gainan Vaisov, the famous religious sheikh and poet who rebelled againt the Russian Tsarist authorities and ended his days in madhouse

I am autonomous; this is my realm;
These are my colonies; I'm at the helm.

You came without the slightest intimation;
You obviously desired your ruination.'

I'll rest my pen awhile and take a bet:
Which one will win? the Dev or Karakhmet?

Who puts his ton-weight finger to the test?
And who throws whom, deploying neck and breast?

My Reader! Be content with what you've got;
Or go back to the Haymarket, if not.

VI

At dawn it's much the same in the bazaar;
The market's brisk; they're trading near and far;

The usual swindles pile on thick and fast,
But all the traders seem a bit downcast.

At every heart a pang of sorrow gnaws.
What is this wave of grief? What is its cause?

The reason plainly is that Karakhmet
Has been a month, and no sign of him yet.

In sadness stood the people of Islam,
When at that moment there appeared a tram.

'What's that?' Far off the dogs all bark and wail;
The tram draws near as slowly as a snail.

Three hours already! Where can that tram be?
It's so far off, it's difficult to see.

'What's happened now?' The market is oppressed;
The Tatars grow impatient and depressed.

VII

As rumour leads to rumour, far away
A furious commotion fills the day.

What is that thunder-clap? Does it not make
The very earth beneath our footsteps quake?

A lion-like roar sets all the butchers swaying.
Or can it be a pack of asses braying?

Perhaps a sandstorm coming from on high.
A diabolic blackness fills the sky.

What is this ringing? Judgement's Day is near!
The world is ending. How the people fear!

A comet sent by Fate comes boding ill;
Hear Azrail's dread trumpet loud and shrill.

It prophesies the death of all around;
The Khan's great mosque may tumble to the ground.

The doors of Heaven slam shut. Ah what forboding!
Or can it be a fat man's paunch exploding?

As if in shivering fever, houses shake.
God's will is strange. How much more can we take?

Inside their boxes boots and shoes are jumping;
While hats and fezzes scatter, thumping, bumping.

And brother knows not brother, friend nor foe:
'There is no Help or Strength', they whisper low[16].

What evil has befallen poor Kazan.
The Fates have sent a curse on every man.

VIII

The moment passed; the clouds moved from the sun;
The dust has settled, gladdening everyone.

The tram draws up, the sign of Heaven's hope;
It's pulling something heavy on a rope.

Can it be true? Has false hope made us blind?
The Dev with fez on head is dragged behind.

---

16 A common Arabic exclamation, *lā haula wa lā quwwata illā billāhi*, 'There is no help or strength save in Allah', repeated in moments of distress and exasperation

The cursed bully screams there in its wake;
He bellows and the earth begins to shake.

His nose is bloodied, but he lives and breathes.
The Severed Head rolls at his side. He seethes.

The tram's been dragging this colossal hulk;
Its speed has been impeded by the bulk.

The Dev hurls curses, turning day to night;
The Muslims shake and tremble in their fright.

But then rejoicing takes the place of dread;
All hear the laughter of the Severed Head.

Brave Karakhmet emerges from the car;
Like some proud lion he gazes near and far.

The Haymarket comes rushing to his side;
This giant who took their suffering in his stride.

And every trader calls to him *Salaam* ;
He answers *Wa Alaikum as-Salaam*[17].

Now everybody rushes, eager yet
To greet the Severed Head and Karakhmet.

Then from the tram a boy stepped down, so fair;
His countenance a thing of beauty rare.

And then *she* came, unveiled, in radiant light;
Could men have dreamt of such a beauteous sight?

By chance, a *Haji*, looking at her, spoke[18];
He winked at her and made a *risqué* joke.

The Severed Head, whom no one could call meek,
Rebuked the pious joker for his cheek.

The *Haji* said: 'I'm sorry. That's not good.'
Great grief assailed his eyes. And so it should!

Then came the Holy *Ishan*, lash in hand;
He cured the Head by muttering something bland.

---

17 The traditional Arabic greeting: assalāmu 'alaikum, 'Peace be on you'
18 Haji: a title taken by a person who has made a pilgrimage to Mecca

The Severed Head became a wise young man,
With hands and feet in place, as was the plan.

It was a miracle; no one was bored.
In fact all bowed their heads before the Lord.

But where's the Dev? He's gone without trace;
And now resides up-town – a smart, new place.

The Severed Head, now turned a smart young man,
Became, of course, a merchant in Kazan.

And Karakhmet, because he acted duly,
And served his people honestly and truly,

Received a fine gold watch, but not a chain.
They couldn't find his size. But don't complain!

Di dum di dum di dum di dum di dum
May God bless our bazaar to Kingdom Come![19]

The Shuraleh[1]

I

Past Kazan into the country
There's a village called Kurlai.
In that village even hens cluck.
God alone could tell you why.

Even though I was not born there,
For a while it was my home.
There in spring I tilled and harrowed,
In the autumn reaped the loam.

I recall in all directions
Lay the backwood's broad delight.
Grasslands there of glossy velvet
Dazzled everybody's sight.

---

19 di dum di dum: in the last verse of the poem the metre is indicated by using the pedantic Arabic formula as a mnemonic for scansion: *fā'ilātun, fā'ilātun, fā'ilātun, fā'ilāt*. This method was employed in traditional Muslim schools, where rote learning was the normal practice. See the note on translation in the Introduction

1 A mythical horned demon, which inhabits the forests of Tatarstan

And is the village large? O no!
It's just a hamlet in a ring.
All its daily drinking water
Comes from one, lone tiny spring.

Neither cold nor hot, its weather
Mild and soft will ever please;
At times it rains, at times it snows,
And sometimes comes a gentle breeze

Strawberries red and raspberries redder
Thrive in plenty in the woods.
In a trice you'll fill your bucket
Brim-full with theses earthly goods.

Marvellously lined in rows
Stand pines and fir-trees, warriors proud;
Amidst their roots I used to lie
While gazing at a passing cloud.

Under birches, under limes grow
Sorrel, mushrooms in a glade;
Lovely flowers bloom and flourish
In the dappled light and shade.

Red and scarlet, blue and yellow
Blossoming in sunlit bowers;
All the world is fragrant from
The heady perfume of those flowers.

Butterflies which love the blooms
Return to find out now and then
How they fare; then flit and flutter,
Off once more and back again.

All at once the birds of Allah
Fill the woods with their sweet song.
Ah, those tunes! They tear my heart-strings;
Up into the sky they throng.

Bird-song outstrips dancing-parties,
Orchestras and sidewalk clubs;
Circuses, theatres, concerts –
All replaced by trees and shrubs.

Like the ocean, vast and boundless
Stretch the woodlands in their breadth;
Like the hordes of Chingiz Khan
No limit to their awesome depth.

In an instant old men's stories
Are forgotten; names, domains—
All those glories of the past!
At present nothing much remains

Then the curtain slowly rises
And our present lot we see.
Alas! Alas! What happened to us?
Slaves of God we too must be.

II

I've talked a little of the summer,
Autumn, winter — that's my style.
What of girls red-cheeked and black-eyed?
Dusky brows can wait a while!

I'll forgo my recollections
Of the Plough-Day, Harvest-Day.
If I mused too long on those things,
I should surely lose my way.

But wait! I dwell on pleasant things
And I may easily go astray.
How could I forget the title
Of this poem is *Shuraleh*?

You will have the tale, my reader.
Have some patience. Be so kind.
When I think about my village,
I quite often lose my mind.

III

You might guess that in those thickets
Many birds and beasts reside:
Bears and wolves, and then the fox
For villainy known far and wide.

Hare and squirrel, moose and mink
And other sorts are often met
By the huntsman who dares roam
The wide, broad woodland with his net.

In those woods, so thick and gloomy
There live demons — so they say:
Ghostly forms like *albasti*
And *ub'r* and even *shuraleh* !

This is the most likely reason
Why those woods are broad and wide.
In this world devised by God
Can any wonder be denied?

IV

About such wonders I shall utter
A word or two, if that I may;
Sing a little, lilt a little—
That's my custom, that's my way.

Once a fellow from the village
Harnessed up and took his horse.
In the moonlight, all alone,
Through the woods he steered his course.

Soon he drove into a thicket,
Heaved his axe and set to work,
Felling trees and chopping branches,
Chipping trunks of bark and cork.

The air was silent and quite chilly,
Usual for a summer's night;
Birds were sleeping in the forest,
Hushed beneath the pale moonlight.

With such calm and clement weather
There in good and cheerful mood,
See our fellow working bravely
In the darkness of the wood.

Axe in hand, he stopped awhile
To wipe his brow, then jerked his head.
A piercing cry within the forest
Filled him with a sudden dread.

Chilled and startled, our poor fellow
Looks and sees a dreadful sight.
Something strange and eerie greets him,
Comes towards him from the night.

What can this be? Ghost or demon?
Fugitive? He could not tell.
Such a foul and ugly creature
As might live this side of hell!

See its nose, hooked like a moose's.
See how from its face it shoots.
Arms and legs all curved and crooked,
Looking more like twigs and roots.

Eyes deep set in burning sockets,
Sparkling, glinting in the moon;
In broadest daylight, even here,
A beast like that would make you swoon

Its feet are bare with bony toes;
Its form like man of woman born.
From its forehead of the size
Of a middle finger sticks a horn.

Then the fingers, thin and narrow
From its hands stretch straight and long;
Ugly fingers like the devil's,
Each of them six inches long.

V

Both began to eye each other;
Then our man courageously
Asked the ugly creature, saying:
'What is it you want of me?'

The beast replied to him: 'Please trust me.
I'm no robber in this wood.
I don't bar the road to people,
Though to some I bring no good.

'I am fond of tickling humans.
That's the practice I employ.
When I saw you in my thicket,
I could only jump for joy.

'Come to me; come closer, fellow!
Let me brighten your sad eyes.
Let us play a game of tickling.
Let us laugh till someone dies.'

'I'll not argue', said the fellow.
'Gladly I shall play, but see
Let me make my own condition.
I've no doubt that you'll agree.'

'Your condition?' said the beast.
'Well, make it now, without delay.
'I shall do whatever's needed.
But for God's sake, let us play!'

'Listen', said the man, 'I'll tell you
What is needed right away.
Over there I want to move
That heavy trunk that blocks my way.'

'I shall help you', said the beast.
The work is hard, but I'll agree.
First we'll load it on the carriage,
Then we'll trust in destiny.'

The woodsman said: 'The work's begun.
I've split the end of the trunk already.
Now can you put your hand inside,
My forest ram, to hold it steady?'

The Shuraleh made no objection,
And obedient as a dog,
Clumsily and awkwardly
He hobbled over to the log.

Into the cleft he slipped his fingers.
Now, dear reader, can you find
The answer to this simple question:
What did the woodsman have in mind?

With the butt-end of his axe
He rammed a wedge beside the hand.
Step by step and knock by knock
His ruse was working as he planned.

The Shuraleh sat by the log
His fingers stuffed into the end.
What the forester was up to
He could just not comprehend.

Finally the wedge dropped out
And then the heavy log at once,
As the forester had plotted,
Squeezed the fingers of the dunce!

The Shuraleh began to howl,
Tried to escape and break away
But how to get out of his trap?
He simply could not find the way.

Then finally he understood
The nature of this clever hoax
Forced to give up all his efforts,
He began to plead and coax.

'Have pity on me. Let me go,
Dear human. Please be kind and fair.
In the future I'll not worry
Your dear kinsmen. This I swear!

'Nor shall I allow the others
To molest your family.
All the other *shuralehs* will hear me:
'He's my brother. Let him be!

'Ah what awful pain I suffer!
Set me free I beg and pray.
Do you really find such joy
In torturing a *shuraleh*?

The Shuraleh was squirming, swearing
That one day he'd play his part.
In the meantime our brave woodsman
Made all ready to depart.

He checked the bridle and the harness
Placed his axe upon his mare.
What happened to the Shuraleh
He did not have the slightest care.

'You are so ruthless. Set me free.
Where do you go? This is no game!
But if you are so hard of heart,
At least tell me your own good name.'

'Well then, listen and remember.
I am called "A Year Ago"[2].
Learn it carefully for the future.
As for me I ought to go!'

The Shuraleh, all writhing groaning
Tried to tear himself away,
As he pondered in the future
How he'd make this man his prey.

He yelled: "A Year Ago! He squeezed
My fingers with a log. What pain!
Now who will rescue me from here?
And who will save me from this bane?

Next morning all the forest cursed him,
Beasts of every shape and kind.
'You're insane', they said. 'You're crazy.
Have you gone out of your mind?

Why disturb the sleep of others,
Howling, yelling, shouting so?
What's the point of telling us
That you were squeezed a year ago?

---

2 An obvious influence of the story in the escape of Odysseus from Polyphemus

MUHAMMAD ZAKIR RAMEEV 'DERDMEND'
(1895–1921)

'Derdmend' 'The Pained One' was born in a village in the Urals to a family of merchants. He studied geology in Germany and was the owner of several gold mines in the Orenburg district. With his brother he founded the first Tatar newspaper, Vakit *'Time', and the literary magazine* Shura *'Council'. His verse, though small in quantity, is now highly regarded. After the 1917 Revolution his property was confiscated, and he died in penury in 1921.*

I could not even sprinkle my pale shroud

Although I lived and breathed among the rest.
I might have been a corpse for my own land.
Yes, I existed there and passed my time,
But I was counted nothing in the end.

Majnun[1], Farhad! They burnt with such desire,
And for their ardour earned eternal fame.
I too was scorched more than a hundred times,
But unlike them gained little from the flame.

> I burnt with such strong passion. All the same
> Not one soul ever stopped to ask my name.

To some comes eminence, to others hope.
The hand of destiny is widely spread.
But I was cheated by the palms of fate.
I never even had a crust of bread

> Some prosper when to them fate tuns its head.
> One crust I asked, but I was never fed.

'He's mad', they used to say. 'A crazy fool,
Who loves his nation. Go, poor thing, and burn!'
At first my face went red, and then turned grey.
I went through life, but nothing did I learn.

> My life passed by, but little did I earn.
> For all my love I failed at every turn.

---

1 Majnun, Farhad: the names of the two most famous lovers of Arabic and Persian verse. Majnūn 'The Mad One' gave his life for his beloved, Laila; Farhād, fell in love with Shīrīn, who commanded him to hew a mountain and bring down a stream from its summit

And oh you Tatar girls! You shining stars
Of my romantic hopes for love so true!
I searched in vain before the sun came up
And never tired. Your charms were always new.

> They never were enough. What could I do
> To satisfy the thirst I had for you?

The winds blew softly from my country's heart;
Their melodies would haunt me day and night.
Yet from their mournful tunes I had no joy;
From those cool breezes there was no delight.

> I listened when the wind moaned soft and light,
> But never once retained a song in flight.

Where is that holy hill? Where is the spring
Of life eternal? Where the sacred source?
I often knelt in prayer, but found no goal.
The tears I shed were tears of sad remorse.

> No aim in life, and no compelling force;
> No hand to guide and to set me on my course.

The blessed water of my nation's spring
Eluded me. I always lost the trail.
Now death draws near; I look upon my shroud.
Unsprinkled there it lies, its cloth so pale.

> My ineffectual hand could not regale
> A shroud with water. Even here I fail.

My only hope is Allah

As I stumbled along the road, I leant and I said:
> My only hope is Allah.
I lay on the earth, my hands at the back of my head.
> My only hope is Allah.

Tainted for ever and sullied in every way
I prostrated myself and fell like one who was dead.
> My only hope is Allah.

At the sound of the horn the caravans made to depart.
I too set out and followed wherever they led.
> My only hope is Allah.

And those at the rear overtook me and trampled me down.
As under their feet I lay in the dust I said:
   My only hope is Allah.

Like a worn-out coat I was patched and mended again;
A garment quite worthless and bare to the very last thread
   My only hope is Allah.

I was cheated by all, ejected and cast aside;
Like hay to the horses and bones to a dog I was fed.
   My only hope is Allah.

Whatever its colour my dress still looked shabby and torn;
My turban was dirty, my cap was a old faded red.
   My only hope is Allah.

Autumn

Summer has gone
The snow and the rain of autumn sets in;
Ice begins to cover the heart of the blue lagoon.
The flower has withered;
On its stem remains a thorn
Ah, nightingale!
For you only a thorn is so dejected.

The ship

The sea roars . . .
The strong wind blows . . .
In full sail the ship goes forth
Day and night
She wanders and roams
Looking for unknown shores . . .
Winds abate
Waves abound
In which direction is our nation hauled?
Which abyss,
Which deadly paths
Beckon to us, demanding our soul?

Sometimes

Sometimes in melancholy I repose
Listening to the stillness of the universe.
A voice resounds in my ears
I say:
— What is it?
— Whence does it come?
In the place of a response
Water purls,
Ivies rustle in the wind.

SAGIT RAMEEV (1880–1926)

Sagit Rameev was born in the Orenburg district, and quickly established his reputation as a rebellious and decadent poet. His journalism led to political persecution from the Tsarist authorities. After the 1917 Revolution he worked as a secretary and teacher. He died in 1926 of tuberculosis.

Deceived

Now all is over, and my soul has died;
All cease to trust my heart; no zest, no cheer.
Each day is hard for me; each night a tomb,
And every day seems longer than a year.

I grow more bitter with each passing day;
I knit my brows before the world's sad plight.
The world deceives; there is no truth at all.
I say: 'It rains.' It lies and says: 'How bright!'

No! In the sky the sun does not exist.
Another falsehood added to the lie!
No moon, no universe! They are not real,
But fantasies which, wrapped in shadows, fly.

Indeed, there are no skies above the earth.
In all this grief can there be any land?
There is no nature; not a human soul,
Alive or dead, exists to hold your hand.

No single thing on earth retains its truth;
This 'no' itself is but an empty name.
And I am finished, cheated, all ablaze,
My whole existence here consumed by flame.

Those joyful times, the merry tunes I played,
Like vanished, rippling streams will not come back.
My nights have joined together in one day,
With smoke and evil fumes made dark and black.

The people of this world in which I walk
All stare at me with ugly, rusty eyes.
And when they see my form they shout and swear;
They curse me to my face with angry cries.

If one confronts another in the street
And sees his business thriving for the best,
A serpent with its deadly, poisoned fangs
At once uncoils itself and stings his breast.

Now turned to stone, this wretched world so mean
With all my spirit I condemn and curse.
The candle bids that lovers drift apart
And with its flame consumes the universe.

But will this hopelessness bring any good?
Or to this darkness will I always cling?
Perhaps the wind might one day turn around
And on its wings sweet warmth to me might bring.

Soviet and Contemporary Verse from 1917 onwards

HADI TAKTASH (1901-1931)

Hadi Taktash was born in the Tambov district of Russia. He first taught in a local village and during the First World War became a journalist in Tashkent and Bukhara. In 1917 he came to Orenburg where he worked for the media. Later he went to Moscow and finally settled in Kazan, where he died before the time of the Stalinist purges.

The angels of death

(a protest against the First Imperialist War of 1914)

He climbed through the mountains, and reaching their summit
He wearily lowered his wings to the ground.
A star on his forehead gleamed bright in the darkness
And from his clear glances the dawn blazed around.
The dawn blazed around him. The world was illumined,
But then came the winds and despondently said:
'Here are graves,
Here is sorrow.
No place for you, Angel.
For here rule the spirits who call to the dead.

And once he had flown to this star to endow it
With fortune; this Eden he decked out with flowers;
He sowed them and tended them, watered them caringly;
Red was the colour he chose for his bowers.
And then he sang tenderly
Songs of the heavens,

Voluptuous songs
And his planet was fair;
A rival of Paradise.
But when he looked again
Places he saw that were stony and bare.
And so once again he went off to find flowers
Again and again
Through the stars of the night
He fluttered collecting exquisite creations
To make his new Paradise perfect and right.

At last he returned,
But alas! he was greeted
With mountains of bones which were whitened and dry;
The oceans were red with the blood of the slaughtered.
The earth had gone mad; flashing steel pierced the sky.
The roads strewn with corpses stretched out in the distance;
The flame of the underworld flourished alone.
His wonderful planet was dark with their scorching
And ashes remained on the earth he had known.

'The house of my joy taken over by madmen!
Ah! Who are these predatory beings? From where
Have they come to plot evil and wanton destruction,
To turn into ashes my Paradise fair?'

No answer.
But only the howling
Of shells filled the air.

He pondered awhile. As he thought of time's passing
He wearily lowered his wings to the ground.
A star on his forehead gleamed bright through the darkness.
And from his clear glances, the dawn blazed around

On a dark night

Through dried out veins deprived of vital blood
At night my thoughts like burning poison flow;
My gloomy fancies roam the distant steppe
Where cold winds howl and icy currents blow.

My fire is spent, my spirit has been wounded
With arrows of predation cruelly hurled.
I wish to die, to go away for ever
From hangmen-devils and their evil world.

Let those stay on who feel they live in freedom.
But I shall go and from this hell depart,
O earth debauched and plagued by greedy serpents
Which swarm in your embrace and choke your heart!

I go as I erase my earthly traces
And in the clear blue yonder disappear;
There I shall soar on high among the heavens,
And curse the grovelling monsters I knew here.

I take my leave, but I shall not forget you,
You who reviled me! Yes, I shall rejoice
To see the way in which your peace is shattered
By the distant wheeze of my malicious voice.

Consolation

1

The wind groans . . .

The wind howls and speaks to me angrily now:
'You were born to this world but were given no place.'
And because I was born without love and religion,
They call me unworthy and laugh to my face.

Who conceived me in tenderness? Where was that love?
And was there no mystery linked to my birth?
Do they know? No one tells me. They leave me to perish
And burning with anguish I go from this earth.

All the men who surround me are evil and deaf;
Their hearts are as cold as the coldest of stones.
They stand in dark crowds and they jeer at me rudely,
Disturb me and cruelly poke fun at my groans.

With the passing of years I have searched for a faith;
I have searched but found nothing I might have called mine.
And now I have even lost hope in my fortune,
The last fleeting shaft of that radiance divine.

The sun gave no light, nor the moon one bright ray
To illumine the goal to which once I aspired.
The stars like magicians, and thoughts born of greatness
Deceived me and all to my downfall conspired.

As soon as I looked upon beauty and joy,
Their light was extinguished and lost in the mud;
Hypocrisy shattered all canons of trust,
And the lies that were sown left their traces in blood.

It seems my existence has drowned in the gloom;
I stand all alone without honour or worth.
Can anyone answer? Can anyone tell me
The reason why was I born on this earth?

2

I was born for the magical words of my songs
To be carried abroad to the edge of the land
Then to shake up the world with their power and might,
For the spirit of Byron revives at my hand.

The day has now come; to the sky of dark life
My tears like the stars purest radiance bring;
From the sound of songs which inspire the whole world
Every corner has bloomed like a garden in spring.

> Then bowing in awe to the call that I make
> The earth and the heavenly firmament shake.

Kazan

There once was a time
When my eyes shone with hope,
But today they are sad
And for joy have no room
For myself I nurse hatred
And feelings of shame
And wherever I turn
I see pictures of gloom.
In earlier days
I was bathed by the sun,
The days of the springtime,
The freshness of dawn;
But the heat of the sunbeams
Has long since grown cold,
And I know not the sources
From which they were born.

Ah Kazan!
It is painful
For me that today
There is nought but betrayal
And lie upon lie.
I once was a rebel
But then went astray
In the swamp of the bourgeoisie
Slowly I die.

Ah Kazan!
It is painful
For me that today
The warmth of my spirit
Is lost in the shade.
The heat of the bourgeoisie
Turns my heart cold
Like a flower in the autumn
I tremble and fade.

Ah Kazan!
It is painful
For me that today

Poetasters are caught
In debauchery's flood,
While the insolent 'Nepmen'[1]
Like pigs with their swill
Grow fat on their diet
Of thin human blood.

Ah Kazan!
I had hoped
For a few likely friends,
But here our Don Quixotes
All thrive and do fine;
While the Nationalists
Stubbornly
Turn a deaf ear
Always shouting and arguing
Drunk on good wine.

Could it be that their squabbles
And little affairs
Will blind me and stifle
My spirit as well?
Could it be that the fire
In my breast will go out,
Which once made my heart
A rebellious hell?

And if that should happen,
Then what should I do?
Kill myself? End my life?
Then from grief and despair

Fling my hopes
In the cesspit of all that I see
And sunk in my suffering
Bury them there?

Oh no! Such a sacrifice
I could not make.
And why should I give

---

1 *Nepmen:* (Russian *Nepmany*): speculators who profited from the National Economic Plan (NEP)

Satisfaction to those
Who created this treachery?
I am the one
Who can break into pieces
The world of our foes.

It is time!
Let us smash up
This mould made of clay.
Its last days are counting
The ultimate sum.
And listen!
The forces of youth
Are on hand.
And nearer
And nearer
And nearer
They come!

ZAGIRA (ZA'IRA) BAICHURINA (1880–1962)

Za'ira Baichurina was born in the Tatarstan village of Tersk, where after finishing school she worked as a teacher. She played an active role as a propagandist during the Russian Civil War, and published her first book of verse in 1922. Her work displays the didactic tone prevalent in early Soviet writing.

Flax

Take the plough and bring the cart out.
Let's plant flax and work the field.
When it's damp the sowing's easy;
That's the law; the earth will yield.

The time has come, so now to business!
See, the yellow flax stands high.
Mind the heads and pay attention;
Harvest-reaping bye and bye.

Lay the flax out in the sunshine.
Let it dry; don't be forlorn.
Sultry heat will bring rejoicing;
Threshing will begin at dawn.

Shake the rattle; spare no effort.
Raise your voices with good cheer.
On that side you lay the fibres;
Keep the seeds safe over here.

Pull the flax out, pretty maidens!
Spin and spin the whole night through.
Sing your songs; your hearts are joyful.
Turtle-doves, you bill and coo!

Turn the wheel and twist the thread round.
Careful lest the thread should split.
Move the shuttle faster, quicker.
If it's dry, you'll have to spit.

Take the yarn and wind the skeins up;
Cut the fibres with your friends.
Tie the threads up with a ribbon.
Careful not to lose the ends!

Rinse the fabric, toss and shake it;
See, the flax is white as snow.
Then you'll sow a frill so dainty,
The boys will never let you go.

If you're making quilts and pillows,
Pull the thread to its full length.
If the threads are counted properly,
You'll succeed and save your strength.

Hit the reed with force and vigour.
Keep it even; hear it ring.
Print the pattern on the towelling.
Every flower brings the spring.

Now we'll sew our pretty dresses;
See, how elegant they grow!
All your days at work were happy.
Red and beautiful they glow.

You've worked hard, and now you're dressed;
Ah, such a pretty, youthful band!
Helpers of your grateful people;
Stars that light the mother-land!

Temptation

Like flour that spurts out from a sieve
My life continued joltingly;
I've suffered kicks and blows enough.
It's mainly taunts and jeers I see.

When someone's lost upon the road
He heads for any light, like me.
I go in search of any roof,
But scorn is what I usually see.

'All I want is your true love',
My friend repeated tenderly.
But I've no money in my purse.
He wanted something else, I see.

The beauty enters some fine house;
In pearls and golden threads is she.
But they weren't got by honest work.
For them she had to sin, I see.

Though life is an expensive gift,
The world is ugly — this I see.
One will deceive; the second begs;
The third endures humility.

I too have been deceived, my friend.
I thought that brass was shining gold.
I looked at silver in the end,
But even that was false, I see.

IFFAT TUTASH (ZAHIDA BURNASHEVA) (1895–1977)

Zahida Burnasheva, who took the Arabic-Turkish pen-name of 'Iffat 'modesty' was born in the Ryazan district of Russia, and educated in a Tatar school for girls. Throughout her life she worked as a journalist and held several government posts. Her first book of verse was published in 1915.

The Volga

To the Volga this heart of mine I compare
For is it not true some resemblance they keep?
Like the Volga my heart is sweeping and wide;
Like the river's strong current it runs so deep.

As the river goes raging and storms in its depths,
Agitated, excited, my heart does not tire;
But sometimes a calm will make it so still,
As if it might never be kindled by fire.

At sunset the Volga is bathed in pure light;
When illumined by love, then my heart is the same.
Like the waves of the Volga, caressed by the sun,
The flower that grows in my heart is the same.

I search

This life has no inspiration,
Like the earth by darkness cursed;
The languishing heart is weary
Like the summer dying from thirst.

The moon shines out in the heavens,
But is that really light?
I pursue my way through existence;
The road is lost in the night.

The stifling heat makes you tired;
The road leads pitifully on.
The flower of desire is wilting;
The new and the holy have gone.

To a lofty, unreachable meadow
With all my soul I aspire,
For I will not stay my footsteps
At a dim and colourless fire.

To the heart

My heart! Why do you ache?
   Why is your fire consuming me?
Does fire torment your being.
   Or are you the fiery sea?

Did God install the flames
   Of Hell within my burning breast,
Or was the fire spooned out
   From you, affording Hell no rest?

My heart! You languish in
   A sack, imprisoned, starved of air.
In vain you flutter your
   Poor wings – a bird caught in a snare.

But why such futile effort
   To forget my true delight?
For if my breast were not
   In flame, my tears would not be bright.

Yet I might shine in joy
   And live in plain simplicity,
If only there were no
   Defiling squalor under me.

I could have strolled through gardens
   Picking tender flowers, and sung;
I might have been so happy.
   If the nettles had not stung.

I might have known the nightingale
   Its trill loud and diffuse,
If the magpie had not cackled
   While returning to the spruce.

I might have caught the gleaming
   Ray, a star brought from the sky,
If banks of clouds had not
   Concealed the firmament on high.

I might have waited countless
   Years for the fire of dawn to wake,
If hope had not first lit
   The flames that make my being shake.

The verse that struck my heart
   Was born of labour and its price.
The feeling was a fountain
   Rescued from the heartless ice.

HASAN TUFAN (1900–1981)

Hasan Tufan was born in the Kazan district where he studied in local madrasas. After working as a miner in Siberia he furthered his education at the famous 'Galia' madrasa in Ufa. His first volume of poetry was published by his friends in 1928. For some time he worked as a magazine editor for Kazan radio, but in 1940 fell victim to the Stalinist purges and spent sixteen years in Siberian labour camps. He returned to Kazan in 1956 where once again he established his reputation as a poet.

Storm, do not abate . . .

I want to swim, I want to wander
The swan bars the way   (Folk song)

I felled the willow, wound the ropes,
I tied the raft's planks in July;
I planned to go off to the right,
But to the left the wind blew by.

The wave on high; no depths below,
And tirelessly I swam above.
Please spare me, depths; O waves be kind!
And take me back to my true love.

The wind died down, but on the wave
A swan had barred the current's swell.
Now we shall never meet again;
Of my sad plight the bird knows well.

Ah! wander, river, splash and dazzle;
The mooring sickens me; but there
A whirlpool eddies. Do not drown me
In the depths of my despair.

The storm

Perhaps no one will come today, and therefore
I scribble a few verses at my ease,
And evening spins its yarn upon the window
While making patterns on the roads and trees.

But what is this? I hear a sudden knocking;
My corner now grows crowded in the gloom.
And like a gale, a hurricane of force-ten,
My best friend came and burst into the room.

He flew in like a storm, a clap of thunder;
The dark-blue dusk was thickening in the lane.
It seemed that he had taken up the rustle
Of the aspens in his Syrkydin[1] domain.

He looked at me with joy and ardent fervour
And said we should relax and change our ways,
As if we had not come across each other
For thirty years instead of just three days.

We read some verses, heightening emotions;
The argument flared up with boiling zeal.
It seemed a dozen Hadis, scores of Hasans*
Were sitting with us in the room for real.

Perhaps we took a drink? But we had nothing.
We had no need of liquor to inspire.
The sober-headed verses of our Taktash
Were quite enough to set our minds on fire.

Our droning voices followed on each other;
It took no glass, no drink to make us reel.
It seemed a dozen Hadis, scores of Hasans[2]
Were sitting in the room with us for real.

And he was laughing, joking, reading stanzas;
The song we both loved well he sang again;
He scattered all my books across the table,
Just as he scattered all my grief and pain.

'A rebel heart is born upon a storm-cloud;
Tranquillity will make its languor worse;
And like a clamorous storm it seethes and rages
Before it pours itself into a verse.'

---

1 *Syrkydin* : a region of Tatarstan
2 *Hadis, Hasans*: i.e. poets like Hadi Taktash and Hasan Tufan himself

But even so we trust and wait . . .

With flowers fresh the earth has strewn
The paths and roads you knew so well.
Those roads grow anxious. Will you come?
Your village has you in its spell.

The swallows chirp above the shutter;
In the garden roses bloom.
How I recall our distant days,
And for myself can find no room!

For you we keep a goblet full;
Our friendly table keeps your plate.
We know that you will not return,
But even so we trust and wait.

But just suppose he comes one day . . .

How many years has May come by
And longed to meet him on his way.
It waits in vain with hopes and flowers;
But just suppose he comes one day.

I know that he will not come back,
Nor this spring nor the next. I see
Once more the maple turning green;
The nightingale too weeps with me.

Our festive table always has
A place kept free for him to stay.
We hope and wait, but all in vain.
But just suppose he comes one day.

The Caspian shore

The Caspian shore – a gloomy habitation;
The hum of well-known songs, the barrack ramps.
Like geese upon the wing in search of pasture,
They cackle and pass by – the season's tramps.

And life has turned them into natural nomads;
They left their land without regret. I seem
To be like them. A narrow field my birth-place,
A boundless heaven poisoned by a dream.

There is no doubt that everyone reviles me:
'Tramp, Tufan! You waste your years in vain.'
What else to do? Here there are lands and waters
Which never hear the rattle of a train.

Here fields and mountain-spurs, intense heat rolling
The depths of a canal – a song is found.
The season's workers, tramps, like black birds gather;
They call each other, digging up the ground.

Not to leave

My heart! You tiny grain of starry dust;
An obscure fragment of some unknown matter.
Whence did you find your wings? What is the source
Of all this happiness and woes that shatter?

To us in times to come may seem excessive
The griefs and fears of love, the holy rites
Which go with worship of our sacred objects;
Immortal lines of verse and their delights.

Let us perhaps leave all this in the past.
Ah no, my heart, you will not change, but thrive.
Smashed by despair or burning with emotion,
I know that you will always stay alive.

Your gift is this: to bring all that is human
And make it clear to some far distant day;
To keep the strength and power of truest feeling;
To love, to burn, to follow your own way.

Tomb

A simple tomb — a crypt was never in my mind.
I lived the only way I knew; I was not blind.

I knew that I was mortal; please, no room for tears!
It was for conscience, not for terror, that I asked.
And when I die, my friends, just burn these poor remains
Then throw my ashes; let them to the winds be cast.

And when my body is consumed in blazing fire;
When shadows lie upon my face for all to see,
Please do not be afraid; take heart and talk so bold
Of all the plans we made for what we hoped might be.

Like particles of dust my ashes must be strewn
And scattered in the air like birds in radiant flight.
Let each one to its own beloved native-land
Return and for itself pick out a nesting-site.

Here dwells my people, not so good with feeble words,
Not too accustomed to bemoan their piteous fate;
But here must be a child whose guileless, simple eyes
Will see the world uncovered in a newer light.

'Tufan who once went through this life, a passing bird,
Drew near to me and warmed me with a cherished word.'

MUSA JALIL (1906–1944)

Musa Jalil was born in the Orenburg district and was educated in local madrasas. Having lived and worked in Orenburg, Kazan and Moscow, he became known as one of the most talented Tatar poets and playwrights. In 1941 he joined the army and worked as a military journalist. A year later he was taken prisoner on the Volkhov front and sent to Germany where he organized a clandestine resistance movement. For this he was sentenced to death and before his execution wrote the famous Moabite Notebooks, *which record his ordeal.*

The first rain

Far in the distant sky the rain approaches;
The earth's bare flesh is torn up by the plough.
The seeds are cleansed and stored, the baskets tethered;
The village aches to start the sowing now.

At last I saw my father on the threshold.
So long I had been waiting for his voice:
'Musa! The horse? It's ready?'

'Yes.'

'Let's go then!
Off to the barn! There's reason to rejoice.'

There just behind the barn the earth had blackened;
Along the strip the winding furrows lay.
The breeze now cool and fresh caressed our faces
And raised the dust as we went on our way.

Palms over eyes, my father scanned the heavens.
He smiled. His secret was already known:
'A good sign, little son!

   The corn will ripen,
If we have rain before the seeds are sown.'

Poet

The whole night long, the poet could not sleep;
Tear followed tear and fell upon his verse.
The gale roared by the window, and the house
Began to tremble as the storm grew worse.

The wind crashed through the door, took up the sheets
Of paper, which were strewn and thrown apart,
And howling in its fury dashed ahead
With anguished moaning, tearing at the heart.

Like mountains on the river stood the waves;
The oak was toppled by the lightning's rush.
But then the thunder calmed and coldness spread.
The settlement lay weary in the hush.

And in the poet's room till morning came
The storm-clouds slept as if they were entranced.
Upon the sheets of paper tossed around,
In quiet harmony, the lightning danced.

At dawn the poet silently arose;
He burnt his night's creations with the day;
He left the house; the wind grew calm and still,
And morning softly reddened far away.

Throughout that night what had the poet written?
What storms raged in his heart? What had been drawn?
And as he left what words came to his lips
Made tender by the redness of the dawn?

The storm may tell his anguish with its roar
And interrupt your slumber in the night.
The clear rays of the daybreak, tempest-born,
Inflame the sky and set the clouds to flight.

My songs

Songs of the heart on the fields of the Motherland!
Rise to the sun like the flowers unfurled.
Measureless the fire and the passion for life in you!
See how you stand upright in the world.

Light of the tears shed glistening with feeling!
You – my existence here on the earth.
Only your death could lead to my oblivion;
But your life – my immortal worth.

With the ardour of the heart into verse I smelted
The mandate of the people burning with flame.
A song to my friend was his glorious consolation;
A song to my enemy was death and shame.

This base temptation sickens and appals me,
Smothering the heart as the petty world turns.
I live from my songs and the truth that is born of them,
The love in their lines which so brightly burns.

Even when departing from life at this moment
These sacred oaths I shall not betray.
The songs, which I sing are a tribute to the Motherland.
My life I bequeath to my people today.

I sang when I first came to life's gushing fountain;
I sang when the war-clouds thundered their strife.
But still hear my song while here looms over me
The cruel executioner wielding his knife.

The song which taught me freedom from the very beginning
Orders me to die like a man, right or wrong.
My life! You sang like a clear, resounding melody.
Death! You must also ring out like a song!

Obsessive thoughts

I die. It seems I die a futile death;
The only reasons — hunger, frost and lice.
I die just like a beggar-woman sprawled
Before a burnt-out stove as cold as ice.

I dreamed that I would die a hero's death,
Engulfed by fire, and deafened by its roar.
But no! A small, cheap lamp, a guttering flame!
I flicker for a moment, then no more.

And what of the fulfilment of my hopes?
Yes, victory! For me the perfect end.
I could not wait. Vain words: 'I laugh and die'!
O no! I do not want to die, my friend!

Have I accomplished anything of note?
And have I lived so long upon this earth?
Supposing that my life had been prolonged,
Would I have given anything of worth?

I never used to think, I could not guess
My heart might shatter, smash beyond all cure;
I never knew such anger in myself,
Such love, such sadness as I now endure.

And only now I fully realise
This heart of mine can be consumed by flame.
I could not give it to my Motherland.
As I depart, what bitterness! what shame!

The last song

In the far-off distance, the land
That I love is unbounded by space;
Around me the prison I loathe
Is a dark and stinking place.

Up there in the sky flies a bird
On the clouds that swirl above.
But here I lie on the ground,
Hands chained, unable to move.

A flower grows at its will;
With its fragrance it gladdens the day.
But I am unable to breathe;
In this prison I wither away.

I have known every sweetness of life,
Its triumphs, victorious and strong.
And now in this prison I die.
I am singing my very last song.

The Bell[1]

One day outside a private block of flats
I saw a boy, no more than three feet high.
He couldn't reach the button of the bell,
And, obviously upset, began to cry.

I went to him and said: 'What's wrong, old chap?
I'll press it for you. You're not very tall.
Just tell me what to do. How many rings?
No problem. One or two?' And that was all.

'No! Five.' he said. I rang the bell five times.
He laughed and said: 'Come on, let's do a run.
The owner of that flat's a nasty man.
You don't want be to messing with that one!

---

[1] This amusing poem was written in the Moabite jail, a few days before the imminent execution of the poet

FATIH KARIM (1900–1945)

One of the best known and most talented Tatar poets, Fatih Karim died in action during the Second World War.

Autumn rain

The dark and hopeless autumn rain
Drizzles, drizzles, never ends;
With hands spread out and lips pursed tight
They stand in silence, my dear friends.

My closest comrade lost his life;
I could not guess, I could not tell.
By Fascist bullets he was shot;
Out on reconnaissance he fell.

Our backs were wet and soaked with rain;
The comrades had no words to say.
The only sound – our doleful spades
That beat upon the pit of clay.

The task is painful. Can I tell
How hard it is? We stand around;
And underneath a strong, young pine
We lay our comrade in the ground.

And silently we dig his grave;
The groaning wind its message sends.
And all the time fine autumn rain
Dizzles, drizzles, never ends.

Snowdrop

This snowdrop found by a soldier
In a gully damp and remote
Today at your home will reach you
With a concise military note.

Just fix it upon your jumper
You'll be pretty and look much better
When leaning over its petals
You begin to read my letter.

Then, my dear, send me an answer
Quite short, but without delay;
An answer just like this snowdrop
Which is pure and peaceful today.

SIBGAT HAKIM (1911–1986)

Sibgat Hakim is one of the most renowned Tatar war poets. In 1986, the year of his death, he was awarded with the Soviet title 'People's Poet of Tatarstan'

Why does war persist in haunting me?

So often I awake from my bad dream;
I lie half starving in captivity.
But now I am not young or even well.
So why does war persist in haunting me?

To war I gave the whole of my sad youth.
It took so many lives that might be free.
But was this not enough to quench its thirst?
So why does war persist in haunting me?

For ages I have had one fondest dream
That fifty years might pass in harmony.
Do I not have the right to lasting peace?
So why does war persist in haunting me?

But no! The earth that breathes in dire alarm
From such bad dreams affords us no release,
In order that no soul should be at rest
When on the earth there still can be no peace.

Go off to England!

They say to me: 'The harvest of your verse
Is rich. Why are you then so loath to show it?
Dear comrade! Travel. Go to England now,
The cherished land of Byron, that great poet.'

My friends! I know that travel is not bad,
But if I go abroad I fear that I
Shall miss my fertile fields and never see
How in the summer ears form on the rye.

When June comes round, then I begin to yearn
For all the beauty of my childhood place.
I cannot eat or drink, just like a horse
That waits in sheer excitement for its race.

'What sort of horse are you? You have no chance.
You're older now, and racing's very tough.
And don't you know the road ahead is rough?
A peasant's nag can lead a merry dance
To some old trotter. Isn't that enough?'

Lebyazhe in the autumn[1]

Lebyazhe in the autumn! See the trees,
A farewell rustle as they lose their leaves,
Dead butterflies – a memory of the past,
And verses on the table stacked like sheaves.

The woods deserted, houses left till summer;
The birches like dead candles lose their flame,
And everywhere you look there are clear signs
That life is short; eternity – a name!

Light and shade

One half of my ploughed field is in the shade;
The other half is always in the light.
In my fate also there have been two hues
As in this field – alternate day and night.

And on the field of life with passing years
The soul conducts a battle grim and stark
To triumph over sloth, to reach the sun
On narrow lines dividing light and dark.

Thirst

To be in love with you, my native land
Is like the torment of persistent thirst.
I never drained the raw wind dry. For me
Of every fate this fate has been the worst.

---

1 *Lebyazhe*: 'The Lake of Swans', known in Tatar as *Akkosh Kule*, where a retreat for writers was built. See Introduction

Why did you then attract me with your charm?
What love condemned me to this fascination?
Can I not live without you for a day,
Exhausted by this thirst of separation?

The torture of such thirst can be so sweet,
A pain inflicted by some unknown hand.
But my reward – a portion of that light,
When light comes flooding through my native-land.

With dim and quiet magic rendered bright,
So inexhaustible that sparkling love;
My native-land! Caress me as I die,
And wet my lips while bending from above.

NURI ARSLANOV (1912–1991)

At times . . .

At times my soul fills with alarm
   And sudden emptiness;
Great questions vex me, and the hush
   Is still and featureless.

Then my salvation is that friend
   To whom I always look,
Who speaks to me and calms my heart,
   My trusted friend – my book.

Don't fight with ignoramuses,
   Because they always know
They have no equal in their field;
   Their knowledge is just so.

I've tried to argue, but I've learnt
   Such contests are in vain.
At times I even turn away
   From the arguments
   Of my own brain.

AHMED YERIKEI (1902–1967)

Sumbul[1]

Fleetingly you passed, dear Sumbul,
By my house upon your way;
Dressed so light with fabric flowing
In the pink of early day.

Breezes freshening the meadow
Gently touched your silken hair;
Underneath your feet the moisture
Of the dew lay gladly there.

Breath of youth and all its pleasures
Made your cheeks red as the skies;
The purity of your clear spirit
Shone in the brightness of your eyes.

The lark was troubled in the morning;
Envy made the thrush forlorn,
When you stepped out in the meadow,
Singing sweetly with the dawn.

Vain my efforts to pursue you.
Sumbul, how for you I long!
Like my youth will you elude me
Always with your ringing song?

The Lacemaker

I make lace from skeins of silk
Beating heart and twisting thread;
Weaving lace from silk so fine
Pricking fingers, aching head.

It's so difficult, so long;
Just like making up a song.

---

1 *Sumbul*: Persian *sunbul* 'the hyacinth' or 'spikenard', which in poetry is compared to the wavy locks of the beloved. It is also used as a girl's name.

I embroider sweet, new words
As the silk falls from the skein;
Blue the shafts of light which dance
To the sound of pouring rain.

Hear the winds sigh as they pass;
See the waving of the grass.

Let my pattern be so fair;
In this work is all my heart.
When the people see it done
Let them marvel at my art.

Let them know it's all for you
And my love is always true.

You and I are not the same

I stop myself then start again.
There is no peace; day follows day.
I blot the paper; look it through.
My life proceeds the same old way.

You have forgotten, I am sure;
I too forget, and time is long.
But I recall — there was a sea;
I was in love; the wind beat strong.

I wrap up warm and take a walk;
I try to lose myself and trudge
The secrecy of midnight streets —
Not an adviser, but a judge.

It fills my spirit with its chill;
And in myself no harmony.
Somewhere the sea moves in its depths,
Remembering me; remembering me.

It laps in darkness on the shore,
But does it know or guess my name?
The stars, the skies are always there.
Just you and I are not the same.

ENVER DAVYDOV (1919–1968)

Love

The one word 'love' brought to my mind
The image of my motherland.
No sweet words suit my mind today;
My tongue is rough; my thoughts are bland.

For you not only joyful songs
Are fitting when I see your face.
My land! With sadness in my heart
I wish to fall in your embrace.

I know that in such times of grief
You will not leave me torn apart.
I weep in anguish as I press
Your grass and flowers to my heart.

When those who think that they are wise
Call you a bride, and stretch their arms,
Do not believe them. Your strict trials
Are dearer than all female charms.

For years I held you in my heart;
My spirit always kept alive
The history of my own dear land,
Its future glory that will thrive.

No secrets, no reserve exists
Between us; our good faith is true;
And no one, nothing in this world
Could make me stand apart from you.

In grief and joy you love your son.
Why flatter you and call you 'bride'?
You have no need of empty words.
You always were; you will abide.

My pen

My pen will not obey my heart
And I myself do not know why.
As soon as I sit down to write,
Its flow of ink begins to die.

Within my heart a new-found flame
Is kindled by the bellows' blow,
But on the paper one sad trace
Of fire extinguished long ago.

A storm of passion grips my breast:
I long for her! But in the end
My pen will scratch: 'I love you like
My dearest sister, or my friend.'

Ah pen! Consume yourself with passion!
Be more open! Play your part!
Guided by such decent caution,
You cannot reveal your heart.

On day the fire will break the skin
Of tight convention. Then once fanned
The flame will roar about your nib,
And lightning will come from my hand.

SAJIDA SULEIMANOVA (1926–1980)

Through the years

The years pass by. Look here's another gone!
It said: 'Farewell! We shall not meet again.'
So sad to see how wrinkles come like threads;
But this is Time unravelling its skein.

Like ice the ball of thread melts with the sun,
And we cannot recall where it began.
I dashed headlong, and never stopped to note
How fast life raced, how speedily it ran.

The irksome years did not pass over us;
It's *we* who travelled on their jarring strings.
Our life is but one taut, vibrating wire;
An epoch is an orchestra that sings.

The tighter every string is pulled and stretched
The quicker bursts the storm of notes on high.
Their echo dwells and fills the memory;
And in the heart their sound will never die.

Their song traverses every earthly space;
It flies against adversities and fears.
It is not time that passes, but *we* pass
And lay our chosen pathway through the years.

SHAUKAT GALIEV (b. 1933)

My generation

The age made no concessions to our childhood;
Just cold and hunger, constant cares and fears.
The war gave no escape, nowhere to shelter;
We had to grow up fast beyond our years.

Things ripen quickly in a cosy greenhouse,
But we were forced to labour from the start.
We learnt about maturity the hard way,
The growing process branded on our heart.

Road

Young boys thrill to see the horizon
Stretched out in the heaven above;
Young girls are excited to follow
The pathway that leads to their love.

Old parents stand close to the gateway,
Just counting the days as they turn;
The best road for them is the highway,
By which their dear children return.

I can suffer any hardship

I can suffer any hardship.
No complaints.
Any labour I'll endure.
No consternation.
I have my magic wand.
They call it
Inspiration.

AHSAN BAYANOV (b. 1930)

By the Minaret

Come, draw close to the minaret;
Fill your lungs and look to the sky!
Dressed in clouds of snowy-white,
The tower strides forth, its head held high.

A crescent moon, a sickle sharp,
It ranges over unknown lands
The lively wind clings to its blade,
The heavens take it in their hands.

Now draped in a shawl of cashmere cloud,
Who can it be? No one can tell.
A pretty, upright Tatar girl
Drawing her water from the well.

I see my mother in your form
Walking through the fertile fields.
How long will you walk? How far will you go?
Your gait to exhaustion never yields.

ILDAR YUZEEV (b. 1933)

Raven

O raven! Even in the winter you do not forsake
The nest that you have made, nor fly away.
You are our closest neighbour, even so you will not build
Your home near places where we humans stay.

In terms of reason you, my birds, are much below us men,
Although you soar upon the highest plane.
But there are times when I look up and see a lofty nest.
'And where is mine?' I think with heartfelt pain.

'Where is that nest, that home, I might have raised up for myself?'
I wake alarmed at night and find no rest.
I look towards the poplar and I find myself ashamed
That I am here and have not built my nest.

The setting sun

It may be that our paths will cross again
As life draws to the ending of its days;
And with the setting sun love may be born
Once more from those last, gentle, golden rays.

And then our children's faces will be touched
By oblique shafts of light from that late sun;
And we shall see the features of our youth:
You in your daughter's face; I in my son.

O greenness of the meadows

O greenness of the meadows! Where are you?
Where do the flowers of the garden lie?
Where is the heavy breathing of the storm,
The rumbling of the thunder in the sky?

The homeland which you loved is far away;
No sooner do you sleep when at that hour
Again comes stealing into your fond dreams
The vision of that bashful little flower.

From way beyond the rivers and the hills,
While moistening the sleep within your eyes,
Once more the patterns that you knew so well
Somewhere in deepest consciousness arise

And in the heart a sudden pinch; the soul
Is stung. Where are you, native-land, my home?
The brittle-willows nurse you in their shade;
Your fancies to the kitchen-garden roam.

Without your beauty how then can we live?
For more than once you helped us through our night
Of misery and torment, little flower,
White-pink your colour, trustworthy and bright.

You shake your head in parting and you dream;
At once your home will summon you and call.
The dream, however deep, will be dispersed.
Potato-flower, so white, so pale, so small!

Ballad of sadness

To give much thought to nature
Is just lazy!
The market's at your service
Every day.
I take the wheel, set off
In rain or sunshine,
But nature bows before me
All the way.

Just look around! A birch-box
On the counter;
A strawberry drips its juice
Into a dish;
And if you're tired sit underneath
The elm tree.
Here's the aquarium –
Look at the fish.

Don't gape! The market place is
Really splendid.
And here's fresh sorrel; make
A soup, or chew;

A caged canary tries to sing
Its heart out,
But it will never sell
Itself to you.

Not willing to grow limp
In water-meadows,
The lilies in a basket
Breathe our air.
For winter we've got snow and ice
In plenty;
The purchaser will never
Have a care.

The market at your service boils
And bubbles.
They bargain, praise their goods
And make their pledge;
The barkers call their wares
The trader's happy.
It's he who over nature
Has the edge.

It goes on everywhere this
Carefree trading.
A fish was taken from its stream
Just now.
That's not so sad; there's no real charm
In nature!
But suddenly amid the
Market's row,

Now farther off and then
A little nearer
The plaintive tune of a *kurai*[1]
Was heard.
Stunned by its poignant sound
They all fell silent.
Alarm spread through the market –
Not a word.

---

1 kurai – a Tatar folk musical instrument, a sort of a flute made of wood

The people looked around
In consternation.
Who comes to haunt them
With his magic song?
They looked around again
And started shouting:
'It's just that foolish singer.
Come along!'

'Where have you come from fool?
Where are you going?'
'From meadows and from groves
I wander by.'
'Come, let us have a tune,
You simple madman!
Hey, crazy fool, come sell us
Your *kurai*'

He was amazed. And I, without
A reason,
Gazed after him and thought:
'Why should he sing?
And from our market why should he
Crave nothing?'
He was not tempted by
A single thing.

The people in the market
Seem enchanted;
They crowd around him, drawn
To him somehow:
'How much for your *kurai*, you
Stupid madman?
Come sell it to us, sell
It to us now!'

Embarrassed, he continues
His sad ballad:
'I'm sorry, but this sadness
I can't sell.'
'Come, fool! Come tell us why
And where you're going.'

'To meads and groves. The time
Is right and well.'

He went but in the hearts of young
And old men
A prick of melancholy
Took its toll.
But soon the petty traders
Started shouting.
Indeed you cannot sell
A saddened soul.

The great bazaar resumed
Its noisy business:
'Buy, sell! I took the wheel
And at my ease
Began to follow. Then I saw
Behind me
A queue of Volgas, Ladas,
Zhigulis.

And here they drive behind
Pursuing sadness,
Along the country lanes through
Woods and bowers;
So many cars and all of
Different colours,
Returning to the grass, the leaves
The flowers.

'And can't you hear the tune?' 'No,
We can't hear it.'
Where is that sadness which we seek?
Who knows?
But then I look through groves
And grassy meadows,
Where waves on silent lakes
Caress the toes.

And sometimes just for nothing
We grow sad.
Perhaps we need a reason
To go mad.

KLARA BULATOVA (b. 1936)

You went astray

Upon the river by the whispering reeds
You flew to greet me like a swan at night.
No need to tell the story of your past;
I know. All is forgiven in my sight.

You went astray; but sometimes when I hear
Such tales from others — how their cruel words jar! —
I close my ears, ignoring truth or lies.
But you are mine; I love you as you are.

You went astray; but it was not your fault.
No need for shame; no need to lower your eyes.
You love the sun; you love the breeze that sings.
A soul that loves such beauty never dies.

You went astray, but friendship will endure;
Our selfless joys cannot be torn apart.
Now come to me and let me with my love
Wash clean the wounds that stain your aching heart.

Do not look down, but listen to my song;
For in its words my flaming passions live.
Do not be sad. We shall forget the past.
Whatever happened then, I now forgive.

RUSTAM MINGALIMOV (b. 1937)

Meditations

Tukai sang songs to me of sweetest joy;
My mother whispered: 'Grow strong, little boy'

    In her native tongue.

The gurgling stream laughed as it raced along;
The black-winged starling burst into a song

    In its native tongue.

My hills would meet me, greet me with a sigh;
With sadness airports often said goodbye

    In their native tongue

The heavens rumbled where the station stood;
And platforms saw their wagons off for good

    In their native tongue.

If then I wish to make my verses ring,
May I not answer you, may I not sing

    In my native tongue?

The river of childhood

I see a droplet in a stream
And memories come flooding by;
I see the ocean with its swell
And I remember with a sigh.

But there can be no whiter geese
Than all the geese that I have seen;
And there can be no softer grass
For nowhere is the grass so green.

My childhood's water was so blue
Cascading down the steep incline;
The Swan King splashed upon the wave
Of distant rivers that were mine

RUSTEM KUTUI (b. 1936)

Swallow

Swallow
    Forked tail
With wings
Clinging to its little frame
How my heart
    Rejoices
In the shelter of its name!

It goes
    Turning somersaults
Does it care
For the depths of the sky?
    Will it crash
And wound itself
In the heaven on high?

Swallow
    One love for ever
Does it think
Of its life and its hopes?
A droplet
    A midge or a sunbeam
Caressed it
On rocky slopes.

Swallow
    A childhood mystery
Ah! How we would love
To know!
Its frail wing
    Dark as the night
Swooping
Now high, now low.

Over the sea it disappears
The day is deep and serene;
Even the trees have frozen
    But no shadow is seen.

ROBERT AHMETZHANOV (b. 1935)

My son take this book...

My son, take this book of autumn days
And look through its pages with pride and care.
The leaves tumble down from the maple tree
Like letters, leaving its branches bare.

And in their light of yellow and gold
I see the colours of all that has passed;
My summers were lit by brilliant days,
But summer is short and will not last.

Butterflies take wing and fly;
Wooden horses jump and shy.

❖❖❖

Elegy

The birds have flown their nest; the house in wrecked;
Eternal soil alone marks its foundation.
Black soil! The time will surely come when I
Shall walk towards my final destination.

I do not crave eternity, my land;
I only ask one favour for my toil:
That you should sprinkle with your gentle rain
My dwelling-place, my last said home of soil.

RAVIL FAIZULLIN (b. 1943)

On Bolgar

The ruins subside, and like an age-old dream
The wormwood rises grey beneath the sky,
And like a band of pilgrims through the vault
Of heaven, a flock of homeless birds flies by.

Through groans and tears – the silence is so deep –
An arrow rushes in its muted flight;
The distant tramp of horses fades away;
A spinning cloud of ashes dims the light.

I am alone; my boat clings to a rock;
No clanking from its chain, no joyous sound.
O air of Bolgar! Brief the fading light,
The steppe, the crescent moon, the ruined ground.

Snow and verdure

Life is passing, years are passing,
Neither smoke nor fire is seen;
In the snow of this foul weather
Winter fields will not grow green.

Verdure long ago was stifled;
White with snow the green became.
In the net of worn-out bodies
Quakes the spirit all the same.

Spring with winter fields is mocking
Your old age as white as snow;
Pale the tears with which the world
Sees its children come and go.

The blind sun of the domes

The blind sun of the domes!
The church's sparkling band!
The grudging tears of old men
For my native land.

A hidden yellow light –
These tears reflect its source.
The domes speak plain to me:
No wit is without force.

To us our land bequeathed
Its ruins, not its halls.
The truth about the past
To the ears of sages calls.

Our legacy is hard.
My land! As time went by
We suffered well enough
To understand Tukai.

The sky

The sky is like a sound, trustworthy safe
For hiding secrets in security.
I've stored away a lot of thing of mine
Which I prefer to store in purity.

But sometimes I reach up and lift the lid
Of my blue box upon the shelf above.
I can't resist, and often have the urge
To open it in front of my true love.

Shadow theatre

The shadow of the back-drop can betray
The actor's role – now old, now young in heart,
Adjusted to his age with sober mind
Or in the depths of passion, torn apart.

The audience is consumed; black flames of fate
Before them, barefoot, naked, twist and dance;
The shadow-play unfolds its poignant tale,
And holds its dumb spectators in a trance.

RADIF GATASH (GATAULLIN) (b. 1941)

Other girls were dancing

Still yesterday the mountain waited cordially
And bathed in silver all the flowers shone brilliantly.

But other glades at dawn displayed their gleaming banks
And other girls were dancing on the mountain flanks.

One time I loved to pluck the ox-eyed daisy, yet
My hand now clasps a sweet damp mignonette.

But other glades at dawn displayed their gleaming banks
And other girls were dancing on the mountain flanks.

Now I rejoice at dawn to see the heavens flare;
The morning breaks; grey rime and hoar-frost on black hair.

But other glades at dawn displayed their gleaming banks
And other girls were dancing on the mountain flanks.

Farewell

With my teeth
I touch the air of your street
I touch it with my hands;

Not only with the soles of my feet
But with all of my body
I cling to its warm earth.

It tears itself away from me
And is repelled by me;
When I kiss its blades of grass
I almost try to hold firm.

Not to my embrace
But deeply to my soul
I planted two poplars
In front of your window.

They rustle, they sway
And reach out to me
With their gentle hands.

Melody of memories

Destiny — made of memories
I understand its name

. . . Its shout, its bitter call
Like a despondent voice
Through long, long years
Like melody rose in the heart
Its shout, its bitter call.

I shall not undo my life;
All follows the given course;
Music with its unheard whisper
Turns the soul around.

Destiny — the voice of recalling;
Not even one sound could be added.

GARAI RAHIM (b. 1938)

Generations

My grandfather ploughed and breathed
The air of the soil he tilled,
Never once sparing his strength,
He ploughed as his own heart willed.
He fell headlong in the furrow
Of the land to which he was tied,
And embraced the earth he ploughed
Before he died.

My father ploughed the soil;
He ploughed with passion and love.
The rumble did not abate
From the troubled skies above.
He fell alone in the fields,
Slain by the enemy's lead,
And embraced the earth he ploughed
Before he was dead.

Earth take also my sweat
Streaming hot from my brow.
Now it is time for me
To sow
And plough.

Oaks of my native-land

My little oaks, now you are grown and strong;
And you support the azure of the sky.
So powerful your branches have become;
Leaves gently rocked by autumn passing by.

I wander through the hazel-brakes alone;
The birds of childhood reel, their song so bold;
I touch the wrinkles of the trunks I knew.
Do you still know me, my dear friends of old?

How do you fare?
　　Do you not ever grieve
For days gone by of friendship firm and sound?
And do our comrades come to meet you still
Amid your leaves now fallen to the ground?

I have come back. The music of farewell
In drying leaves resounds and lingers yet.
They sing forgiveness,
　　Memories,
　　　　Promises.
Remember me, lest once we should forget.

Root

My aspirations do not reach the sun,
For life is in this tree, its leaves, its shoots,
And glorious flowers.
　　I do not forget
My origins lie in the breed of roots.

Young girls and children all for beauty wait,
And old, old men await the self same thing.
How noisy it becomes when flowers bloom,
And fragrances are born to scent the spring.

I hear the praise that others make of them.
A root can hear, though deep within the ground.
A wave of rapture shivers through the trunk.
I lie content where hush and joy abound.

In golden darkness
　　See what joy is mine!
Fermenting juices through the rich earth race.
The tree breathes gently
　　Pouring out its sap,
Enlivening the whole world's radiant face.

And I am proud of my unhurried work,
The quiet calm, the slow and peaceful hours.
In spring I know the reason for the noise
Amid the boughs now giving birth to flowers.

On a bus

You turn your head and think: 'O what a fellow!
He's staring, and there's nowhere I can go.'
But you, my dear, could hardly understand it.
My living heart was wounded long ago.

You see, it's you who happen to remind me
Of her, my love, when I was young and free.
Existence without aim or hope eternal –
You cannot know how hard it is for me.

I was in love, and oh! I loved her madly,
And to my love her own response was true.
But all those golden days we spent have vanished
When we could think of starting life anew.

We were the same, well matched with one another,
But headstrong, and there was no give or take.
Perfectionists in love, my dear, we never
Forgave the slightest error or mistake.

The road we took by destiny was chosen;
Because of doubts, the hustle of the day,
I took the right-hand path and then I lost her;
My 'pain' turned left and went the other way.

We separated, and it was so final;
We chose our course content to stay apart
At times, like lightning, love would flash between us
Between two poles of each far distant heart

And you, my dear, are really so much like her,
Much more than it is possible to be.
The flow and ebb of life continues always.
The love I knew will never wane in me.

I might have found some joy, just for a moment;
I might have calmed my heart. I do not know.
You turn your head and think: ' O what a citizen!
He's staring, and there's nowhere I can go.

Still here the snowy fields . . .

Still here the snowy fields, desires of life,
Compassion, weeping eyes, the smiling face.
My youth at its departing waves farewell,
The horses of our fate and fortune race.

They do not tire; the race becomes more swift,
And in the haze above the feather-grass
A mother's tenderness, the fount of love.
The horses race, the earth revolves, things pass.

Now all is left behind and rolling back.
The years, the days we set our hopes upon;
Your crystal voice, your eyes, your brightest glance,
Your pretty girlish form — where have they gone?

The horses of our fate and fortune race.
However much is left, whatever room,
At every moment rises in my path
The granite stone above my father's tomb.

RENAT HARIS (b. 1941)

Windows are the brightest eyes of houses

Shamil Anak[1]

Window casings

The rumbling of the storm, the raging mist!
Above my little window sits a bird.
It flaps its wings and seems to have no fear,
As if the tempest's violence goes unheard.

It neither fears nor frightens anyone;
And unconcerned, oblivious to the rain,
It stays so calmly in the nest it built
Above the casing on the widow pane.

What kind of bird?
   A sparrow, tender-sweet?
   A dove?
   A little cock?
     Well that might be.
But in its head there hide the deepest thoughts
For anyone who has the eyes to see.

Unhurriedly it cocks its head and hears
How nature causes havoc, mends and mars.
And as the weather rages it might see
The freedom-loving soul of the Tatars.

Our windows at the break of dawn grow bright;
Their radiance increases more and more.
And so far only people with pure hearts
Have come this way to knock upon our door.

---

[1] A Tatar poet who lives in Bashkortostan

The felling of the elm

I thought that it would yield at once
With one clean blow;
I heaved the axe against the elm
With all my might.

The meerest shudder rocked the tree,
No more than that.
And from the axe the sparks flew up
In glorious flight.

And I was livid, quite beside
Myself with rage.
Once more I hit and drove the axe
To maim and hurt.
I hacked the trunk; I knew that I
would fell the tree,
But saw its thick, brown blood
Upon my shirt.

There must have been a thousand wounds
Upon the trunk.
A blow, another blow and yet
Another blow.
At last the handle of the axe
And nothing else
Remained and for my toil I had
No more to show.

There was no point in keeping such
A useless thing.
I threw it out among the piles
Of rubbish-sacks.
And in the yard it lay beside
The wounded elm,
A rabid wolf which bared its teeth
And gnawed the axe.

I touched a cloud

Once on my balcony I gently rose
And touched a rain-cloud, hoping it might yield.
I squeezed till there was no more moisture left,
And took the water to my thirsty field.

The torrid cornfield's crop was saved from death;
The wheat would now survive, all would be calm.
My action was indeed a righteous one;
I proudly raised my hand and spread my palm.

I saw my open palm and lost my tongue;
With brown metallic powder it was dusty.
There must be so much metal in the sky
When even clouds which bear the rain grow rusty.

AHMED 'ADIL (b. 1942)

Doves

The city has fallen
   into darkness.
   Night. With its gentle
   touch the wind
   rocks the lanterns.

Some insignificant artist
   maybe
   for the first time in his life
   has painted doves,
   white doves
   on the pavement.

The painter must have
   fallen asleep hours ago,
   but the doves fly on,
   and they will fly
   until the rain washes them away.

But those which he keeps
   in his heart
   will never be washed away
   neither by the rain

nor by time.

MUDARRIS AGLYAMOV (b. 1946)

Ah! Why Creator?

My grandmother was strict, and often said
That we should not disturb the Lord in vain.
Her lessons were effective for a time,
But then we soon forgot her old refrain.

We suffered from the wilfulness of youth;
But teenage years are not among the best.
It happened that our mother passed away,
And soon our father too was laid to rest.

We marked the seventh day of mourning. Then
My grandmother was broken, she would sigh
And moan. We heard her muted words of grief:
'Ah! Why, Creator, did you take them? Why?'

With tears she made her harsh reproach to God;
And that seemed strange to us. She too was weak.
It did not take us long to share her tears:
'O Lord!', we cried. We gained the right to speak.

ZULFAT (b. 1947)

Horses bathing

Horses race like hope while they are still alive,
And like our hopes they do not spare their strength at all.
They race and race, without a pause, without a thought,
And even take no pleasure from the Great Khan's stall.

Who drives them on? Alpamish[1] with his powerful arm.
Who spurs them to the mountain ridge? The Shuraleh.
Who gallops, pulling up the bridle? Human joy?
Or men's misfortunes galloping and holding sway?

The hooves that kick their frenzied beat can shatter stone;
Then flowers spring up and blossom where they left their trace.
The billowing of their flowing manes gives birth to winds;
The winds dispel the clouds and to our fate gives chase.

O groaning air! Are you now sated with the dawn?
The dew so heavy that you bent the willows low?
Fairy-tale horses swim across the raging Ik[2],
Blacker than the blackest tar, as white as snow.

Flight of the soul

Through banks of blackening cloud, the darting bird
Falls like a hurtling stone towards the ground;
A flutter of the wings, no trace of fear,
It shoots up looping furiously around.

And then it courses through the heavenly void,
Now sliding, now ascending to the sky.
Beware of the horizon, little bird,
As you go measuring the vault on high.

---

1 Alpamish: the mythical hero
2 The Ik: a river in eastern Tatarstan

RAZIL VALEEV (b. 1947)

Fire in the Museum of Local Lore

The dawn in its glory breaks over Kazan;
The museum of Local Lore is ablaze!
It burns with the heat of our ancestors' home,
The house we were once more intending to raise.

The flames melt the pearls of our history so old.
And yellowing manuscripts curl in the glow.
We're taking the books to the cellar downstairs.
Lest our folklore end up in the hands of the foe.

These books of antiquity, threatened again
By the greed of the fire which is out of control,
Are covered with soot from the ashes of time,
And their pages, so brittle, are blackened like coal.

The windows are open, and billowing smoke,
As it drifts through the neighbourhood, raises a shout:
'The Museum's on fire! The Museum's on fire!
From all madness and mayhem our trusted redoubt!'

The flames with their howling and bellowing roar,
The fire we were trying to quench runs apace.
My land and my people succumb to its rage,
As it threatens the spirit and soul of our race.

Our history knows ashes and fire well enough;
Our land knows destruction, but goes on to thrive;
And time after time it has risen anew.
The buildings have crumbled, but we're still alive!

We've emerged from the fires that were kindled by time.
In the cellar downstairs our great history reposed
Like the books we have rescued. And, therefore, my friends,
Our Museum of Folklore is temporarily closed!

Heathen

I walk without God and without the Quran;
I wander alone with the distance in sight.
In spring like the leaves my shirt is bright green;
In the winter like snowdrifts its colour is white.

I do not believe in the stories I hear,
But cascading sunbeams suffice with their spell;
I shall look for my Paradise here in this life;
In the very same place I shall come across Hell.

I investigate speech in the streams of the woods;
In the fields I learn patience while walking along;
I am not in a hurry to utter my words,
And never in haste do I make up a song.

There are experts enough. Just be silent and hear!
A nightingale sings and I pause for its sake.
I sleep but its song still flows into my soul;
From my slumber I wish I might never awake.

I bow to the aspens and birches so tall;
I would take the whole forest in one fond embrace.
As the leaves gently rustle, I feel I am one
With the joy of the sound which brings smiles to my face.

O yes! I am no doubt a heathen. I laugh
As I stride to the edge of the world without care.
'Now where is my death?', I call loudly and long.
But only the echo resounds in the air.

The birds in the heavens fly free and unchained;
The stream calls invitingly: 'Come swim and dive!'
And harmony links every atom with sound.
Be forlorn or be joyful, but ever alive!

ROBERT MINNULLIN (b. 1948)

The Wave of the River Syun

The air from the sea! The air with its wonderful smell!
The waves of the sea! The waves of the rippling dune!
I stared in a trance at the ocean's enormous expanse,
And there saw the billowing wave of my own River Syun.

It ran to caress me and offer its tender embrace;
It spilled on the shore, now coming, now running away.
'O, see how life carries us onward and onward!', it laughed,
'And wave follows wave without end just as day follows day.'

I cannot restrain my anxiety; here on my cheek
The salt from the sea leaves its trace; or are they my tears?
I look in confusion, and call to my own little wave:
'I almost forgot how you were in these long, long years.

Your taste and your colour, your sadness I almost forgot,
But here in the depths of the sea when I saw you once more.
My river I knew and remembered each billow by heart,
As the waves of the sea one by one made their way to the shore.'

It gave me no answer; in silence it lapped and it rolled,
And then it was lost in the myriad waves of the sea.
I start once again, Ah! If only, if only it knew
All the anguish I feel, all the pain it has given to me!

How vast is the ocean! How vast its unending expanse!
My river runs free and the waves of the Syun never halt.
But here in my soul is the burning of bitter remorse,
And here on my cheek there is only the trace of its salt.

FANNUR SAFIN (1948–1992)

Snowdrop

My snowdrop! How frail and tiny you are!
Where do you hurry to, where do you go?
You linger a while in the pools of thawed earth,
Amid the blue islets surrounded by snow.

So fresh and so kind like the bloom of first love,
You flower in the cold without terror or fear;
You open your petals, renewing our hopes
For the seasons to come in the following year.

But why do you hurry, my brave little flower?
And will you not wait for the start of the spring?
And can you not stay for a moment to hear
The birds in the sky when they make the woods ring?

RAVIL BUKHARAEV (b. 1951)

Bee

I am sitting here and writing with a ball-pen;
To the window-pane above I turn my eyes.
In the porch outside a hazel-tree is blooming
Like a little yellow cloud upon the skies.

The pollen hangs so heavy on the branches,
A brook runs babbling through the deep ravine;
A bee crawls over my blue sheet of paper,
A wild striped bee that haunts the forest green.

Outside the bee has gone from flower to flower;
I carefully examine it and see
How it has stained its wings and its proboscis
With pollen from the flowers on the tree.

Indeed it has been working very wisely,
Collecting every drop of nectar there.
I must return to my blue sheet of paper,
So I release the bee into the air.

Working in a lonely house takes patience;
How long we need to wait to have our wish
For lines of verse like clear, transparent honey
To shine and sparkle on an empty dish!

For Product Safety Concerns and Information please contact our EU representative GPSR@taylorandfrancis.com
Taylor & Francis Verlag GmbH, Kaufingerstraße 24, 80331 München, Germany